The Rocks Cried Out

Autobiography of a God-Seeker

Bradford Henshaw

Also by Bradford Henshaw
Broken Angel

DEDICATION

Steve Hastings, who spoke to a wayfaring stranger
Wally and Beverly Walrath, who opened their hearts and home
Patrick Ballard, a gentle remembrance

Seeker 1971

Rev. Bradford Henshaw 1981

PREFACE TO THE FIRST EDITION

As a young man, I feel definitely led of God to publish this story of what He has done in saving my unworthy soul. What follows is not a history of me at all but is a story about God: God's dealings with a particular sinner, His love and patience with that sinner, and His unerring faithfulness in leading one lost sheep into the fold. That I happen to have been that sinner is irrelevant, except for the fact that what went on in my mind and heart as God was dealing with me can only be told by myself.

In Christian Victory,
Bradford Henshaw
Goderich, Ontario, Canada
February 2, 1983

"And there are also many other things which Jesus did, the which, if they should be written every one, I suppose that even the world itself could not contain the books that should be written. Amen." — John 21:25

PREFACE TO THE SECOND EDITION

In reviewing THE ROCKS CRIED OUT for this 2013 edition, I see that it was good to have published the story while still in my early thirties. If the zeal of youth causes the story to be rendered with a certain lack of caution, then so be it. I am now sixty five. It is a joy to find a bit of youth salted away in these friendly but harrowing old pages.

Still in Christian Victory,
Bradford Henshaw
Fruitland, Idaho
February 2, 2013

Table of Contents

FOSSILS

Fossil: "The petrified remains of plants and animals which occur in the strata of the earth's surface and are out of harmony with present time and circumstances."

The poetry which occurs in the strata of this book is selected from material which was written by myself and placed into the narrative at the approximate times of their composition. These are inserted to give a clearer look at what was happening in my mind and heart at the time.

The two songs, THE ROCKS CRIED OUT (below) and GLORY MOUNTAIN (following chapter 14) were written since I became a Christian.

THE ROCKS CRIED OUT

I have no holy heritage, was never held by saints
I never heard the hallowed calls around the throne of grace
I never saw my loved ones kneeling in the holy place
I hungered though for righteousness and sought the Savior's face
Until the rocks cried out.

There is a God in Israel but I was blind to see
While I was yet a child of hell He gave His Son for me
He looked the whole world over from His home in Galilee
And when He saw my hungry soul He died on Calvary
And then the rocks cried out.

My mountain broke in pieces all in a great strong wind,
The earth began to tremble for the burden of my sin
I felt a holy fire and my soul began to mend
And after that a still small voice said, "My son, enter in,"
And so the rocks cried out.

Praise ye the Lord, and to His Name
Be all the glory, be all the fame,
Glory be to God in Jesus' Name.

Chapter One

THE STILL SMALL VOICE

The Huntington Beach Pier is a massive structure, a giant Parthenon to the West Coast, reaching out into the Pacific Ocean. Four powerful ranks of columns march out to its tip supporting the long hardwood decking, bleached grey by years of sun and salt.

One summer afternoon, as a teenager, I carried my surfboard down across the sand. Swallows darted back and forth to their mud nests high up under the concrete trusses. I pushed out and stroked across the shadows of the columns. Waves rolled under me with grace as I made my way outside. Forty yards ahead of me a youth with walnut skin came blasting out of a nine-foot peak. Sliding toward me on my left, he traversed the face of the breaker with the agility of a skier. As I rose up to meet him on the wave he reared back, shooting his board over the crest above me. The tremendous wave hissed through the pier like a steam engine, thumping against the pilings, sending spray high into the breeze. My board shot through the peak and eased down the back and I stroked hard, with my whole arm, down through the trough and over the next monster.

Almost to the end of the pier, I took my place among the surfers who were waiting for position. High above, on the pier, fishermen with buckets and camp chairs looked like tiny people out of a storybook. Some were leaning on the iron rail, while others tossed heavily baited hooks over into space. Hot sun dried my back as the gulls drifted lazily on a blue afternoon.

A swell passed under me and a boy younger than I paddled with it. Arms raised in balance he slid away until only his head and hands remained in view above the mass of water. He turned toward the pier, racing directly at the pilings without reserve; then just before he would have smashed through the columns like a rag-doll, he gracefully kicked out and paddled back outside. He had not even gotten wet! As the next wave lifted me silently over I was forced to admit that I could never do it. I knew this eight-foot surf was way out of my category.

I began to feel conspicuous floating there in that little group of surfers. They all seemed to know each other and between rides they would describe the waves they had just ridden, laughing and pointing freely. Trying hard to appear calm and deliberate, I paddled away, determined to get a good distance from them before I dared even try to make it to shore.

Quite a ways from the pier I could see the waves peaking strongly and so I decided to try to ride one out there by myself, unobserved.

The waves of the Pacific usually run in sets of nine or ten, building consistently until the last two or three in the set finish with a climax. I let two full sets go through as I rested and positioned myself for takeoff. The pier lay across the horizon to the north. I could still see the surfers, but it was far enough that I felt secure in my own company.

Three ridges of water advanced out of the sea. I took a few strokes for a better position.

What I didn't know, was that I was in a notorious rip-tide area that was off-limits to swimmers.

The first swell was larger than any I had ever ridden, but I let it pass under my board. My position was good. I figured the last wave to be over eight feet. Before the sea under me began to tilt I was on my knees paddling; then as if the whole earth suddenly rose and my surfboard began to slide off I was into the wave. I stood to a crouching position but before I could get my weight over the rear of the board I watched its nose cut into the clear water at the base of the breaker. Diving out ahead of the board as far as I could, I curled up into a ball and hit the water, the crushing wave came down hard, driving me beneath the surface. It sounded like a roaring waterfall as I hugged my knees in the spinning darkness. When I finally came up, the surface was bubbling with foam. My first thought was for my board. I scanned the shoreline which seemed miles away, dotted with sunbathers and beach towels. A turquoise flash shot up in front of the wave I had wiped out on. I knew it would only be a matter of seconds before it would be washed up on the beach.

If I wanted to be alone, I had definitely achieved it. I felt like a speck floating on the deep. I knew I was in at least thirty feet of water and I began to swim shoreward with abandon, trying to drive dreadful thoughts from my mind. Tiring quickly, I stopped for breath and decided to attempt to body-surf the next five footer.

I swam hard with the face, kicking for all I was worth, but it was no use; without fins I was practically helpless in that powerful tide.

I was tired. The waves continued to build and were soon breaking over my head. My energy was ebbing. When the set had finally gone through I began to swim shoreward, but I was acutely aware that I was doing little more than flopping my exhausted arms before me. The waves were untiring though. Foam buzzed in my ears as I tried to rest on the surface, but before I could relax I was under another rush of foam. That went on until all concept of time was lost and I was drifting into a dream-like condition.

Then I spotted the old couple ambling down the beach. "Help!" I screamed, "Help me!" They looked toward the waves. "HELP!" I waved my arms, "HELLLP!" They must have thought I was kidding. They looked out at me with a sort of wonderment, as though I was some young prankster pulling their leg. I was frantic. I screamed again before ducking under a wall of foam. The last sight I got of them, they were walking down the beach arm in arm.

"Oh God!" I looked up to the sky. "OH, GOD . . . HELLP MEE!" I cried above the surf.

White water. I barely had time to catch a breath before I was washed beneath the surface again. I was crying. It was so unbelievable; the California sun was shining, the beautiful Pacific was rolling in, the afternoon was at its apex, and I was drowning.

When I hit the surface my head was full of water, my heart thudding desperately. I started to cry out to God again, but before I could utter a sound I was under the relentless surf. It seemed comfortable to just hang there in the darkness, but a small voice kept insisting, "Kick. . . kick up. . ." Remotely my feeble legs responded and I was surprised to find the surface inches above my head. I leaped into the sunshine, blowing carbon from my burning lungs.

The beach looked closer than ever. Surely if I gave it every ounce of strength in my very heart and soul, I could make it. In order to know the depth I dropped down with my arm stretched above me. When I touched the sand, my hand was at the surface. I launched out, positive that I would soon be able to touch bottom and rest. I swam, the white water rushed over me, and I swam on.

I fought. I kicked. I pulled out every bit of energy. Then I reached down with my foot, confident I would touch bottom before my head went under; but I descended into a deep black place without any bottom at all.

I had been deceived. When I had checked the depth before, I had touched on an underwater sand dune. Now, although closer to shore, I was in much deeper water. I was sure my lungs would burst. Somehow I found the surface again and screamed into an empty sky for someone to save me. All my energy was gone.

White water rushed over my head. Before I could cough the brine out of my throat, it rushed through again. I thought about the surface. Then I gave up. I had no strength left.

A numbing, restful sleep crept slowly through my body. A deep, far-away ringing seeped into the back of my skull, and needles of light fell through my fading consciousness. I could still feel my heart off in the distance hammering steadily. My lungs were locked.

The ringing in my head gave way to a droning, like B-52's in the night.

Weightlessness.

A squadron.

Then the roaring melted into something like the strain of swarming flies; swarming noisily as they did in the outhouse behind Grandpa's mountain cabin. The grey outhouse stood down the rocky path in the pine trees.

The distant pounding of my heart began to blot out the sky.

The pine trees were fading.

With calm resolve, my spirit reached out to God. He was right there, just above me.

But the buzzing of the flies became the buzzing of the foam at my ear. The natural buoyancy of my inflated lungs had lifted me like a sleeping baby back to the atmosphere. A flash of hope shot through me and I sprang. I was in the surf. Just before the white water hit me I laid my arm across a maroon and gold surfboard. Its waxy deck was against my cheek. The glaring sunlight danced on my vision, I was not dreaming. The boy floating beside me was grinning.

"Do you want to paddle in?" he looked like an angel. "I could swim from here."

"No," I breathed. "I. . . I. . . don't think. . . I can."

Far up on the beach he and his friends had a fire going. I

fell down in a knot with the side of my face against the sand.

§§§

I cannot honestly say I was heathen. I attended a nominal Sunday School as a child, although about all I remember was the big white steeple reaching into the morning sunshine. We put on a skit for the parents one time; I recall standing by a rose-colored curtain in line with a bunch of kids I didn't know very well. I felt like a stranger — it seemed I always did.

When I was twelve years old my father moved the family from Phoenix, Arizona, to Bakersfield, California. I made friends with two brothers, Robert and Steve. They took me to church with them now and then. It was a bit strict; they couldn't go to movies nor dances and their parents didn't smoke nor drink. They never could get me very interested in it.

One night Robert invited me to what he called a youth rally. After the sermon, an altar call was given. I had no thought of going forward, but something was going on deep inside me that I didn't know how to cope with. Everyone was standing. They were singing "Just as I am, without one plea, but that Thy blood was shed for me..." My ears were ringing and I could hardly breathe.

Robert nudged me, I thought I was going to die. He put his mouth near my ear, "Wouldn't you like to go, Brad?"

I gulped, my heart pounded desperately. Before I had time to think it over, I was heading down the aisle. I was taking one of the greatest steps in my life, and I was scared.

We stood around the altar watching the preacher as he pressed the invitation. When not one more soul would come forward, they ushered us back through the halls and into a large bright room with a kitchen at one end. A young man knelt beside my chair. He gave me some papers and little booklets, trying to explain their contents. I never could remember what he said.

When I got home I read carefully through the literature. Somewhere in those papers I was sure I would find the joy of salvation they had spoken of that night. It was not there. Disappointed, I sat at my little desk in my bedroom. Surely, I thought, there must be something to this religious business. Surely Jesus did save people as I'd always heard He did. I dropped the

14

papers in my waste basket and climbed into bed.

That night the Christian religion became a dead issue to me.

§§§

After high school, I attended the junior college in Bakersfield. I wanted to go to California State College at Long Beach more than anything else in the world, but my grades were not high enough. Finally, in 1967, after two years at Bakersfield College, I was accepted for a double summer session at Long Beach State. If I could bring my grade-point average up enough that summer, I would be admitted into the coming fall term; if not I would have to return to Bakersfield and keep trying.

While staying in the boys' dorm in Long Beach that summer I was introduced to marijuana. I had become a bit of a drinker during my years at Bakersfield, though never in my wildest dreams had I considered smoking pot. But a dark-eyed girl from New Mexico influenced me, and before the summer was out I was in the dope dens of Southern California seeking my own personal stash of marijuana and hashish.

At first I smoked dope for the fun of it. It was just a high, another kind of drunk. But very soon it started becoming a lifestyle and a philosophy. The way I viewed the world and my relationships with it were being re-evaluated and modified almost daily. I sensed something was happening in me but I couldn't put my finger on it; I just felt looser, freer, more liberal and progressive at my heart level. I was living away from home for the first time in my life and suddenly there were no bounds to what lay available to me.

I had been getting high on marijuana with Terry, the girl from New Mexico. Some of her friends were becoming my friends. I finally decided I needed my own bag of pot, and so through a friend of a friend I arranged to be introduced to a guy who sold drugs.

I was scared stiff. We pulled up the gravel driveway and parked between an old white house and a seedy looking tool shed. To my surprise we knocked at the door of the tool shed rather than the house. A scrawny, long-haired guy about twenty peered out from the darkness. He squinted at me standing against the sunset, and then he recognized the guy I was with. "Oh, it's you," he said. "Come on in."

It was dark inside and heavy with the smell of incense. There was a dim lamp on the floor in the corner that revealed just enough of the tiny room that one could manage without groping with his hands. The room was no larger than eight feet square, just enough space to sit in a semicircle on the floor facing his stereo. The walls and low ceiling were painted flat black and wild colorful posters were tacked all over.

I was commenting on the uniqueness of his place and trying to relax. In the conversation he told me that years ago, before the city had grown up around his father's little farm, the shed had been a chicken coop. There was a black opening like a small door leading into another area where he said he slept.

The guy I was with told the dweller of the chicken coop that I wanted to buy some grass and the conversation turned naturally to me: where I was from, the college, and so on. Then, as I would later learn was customary, the dealer lit up some of his stock and handed it over for a smoke. As we passed it between us he turned off the little light. Then he switched on a black light and jacked up the volume on the stereo system. We were suddenly sitting in total blackness facing the psychedelic posters which had literally come alive under the black light and appeared to be standing freely in space. By the time we were finished smoking, I had traveled over, under, around and through those posters by way of an infinite universe of three-dimensional art and electric music.

Finally the black light was switched off and the old lamp came on in the corner of the coop. The deal was negotiated under the roar of the music. As I was handing him the money, a knock came on the door and my brain exploded into fragments. Cops! Police! FBI!

He quickly turned the music down and I stuffed the bag of pot into my jeans pocket. He peeked around the door for a moment and then stepped out leaving it open. The dusk was almost gone. From the blue darkness outside I heard the voice of a woman. He reached back through the door and flipped on a porch light. Then I saw his mother, an old farmer's wife.

"They're just some friends, Mom," he answered.

We stepped out into her back yard. She recognized the guy I was with and then her son introduced me as a student from the college. It was very evident that he was pleased to be presenting me to his mother as I appeared so clean cut and no doubt quite different from the usual group that hung around there.

As we pulled out of the driveway and off into the city lights a great wave of relief swept over me. I settled back against the car seat and rejoiced to be safely away from my first meeting with a dope pusher. It would have been impossible on such a fine summer evening to have imagined how deep into that very environment the strange and twisting paths of my life would eventually lead me.

§§§

My grades at Long Beach State rose a little that summer, but not enough to permit an entrance into the regular fall term. I returned to Bakersfield College and home.

One of the courses I took that fall was Philosophy, in which I had to write a term paper. For my subject I chose to research a French cathedral in the small town of Chartres, some sixty miles southwest of Paris. The thing that made Chartres so important to philosophy was that although it had been initially constructed in the early Gothic period, it had burned and had been reconstructed several times through four centuries of powerful change. Each reconstruction and addition reflected the political, economic, social and spiritual conditions of its respective era, producing not only a beautiful connection of architectural styles, but also a masterpiece in human development right through the Renaissance.

I have no idea what it was that caught my spiritual attention. I sometimes wonder if it was the numerous statues and reliefs of Bible characters that graced every doorway and portal. Maybe it was the Bible stories from both Testaments that are told in the hundreds of stained-glass windows. Or maybe it was just the fact that God knew on that winter night, with my nose in a philosophy term paper, I was ready to hear His still small voice. Out of the heavens came a voice that I perceived with my spiritual ear as clearly as any voice I had ever heard, a voice and a message that so changed my way of thinking that to this day I have never gotten over it. I knew instinctively that it was the voice of God.

17

"I AM," said He. "I am God. And you, Brad, must come to know me in this life."

Chapter Two

LUCIFER SATAN DEVIL

I was finally accepted into Long Beach State in the Spring of 1968. One of the first friends I made was Joe. We were both majoring in art and had some classes together. By the time school recessed in June, we were becoming close friends but I found myself drifting farther away from the two guys I was sharing an apartment with. They had been opposed to my dope smoking since the day we started renting together, and when I tried growing my own pot in my room they got hostile. After final exams were over, they kindly asked me to find new accommodations.

"It's not that we don't like you, Brad," Carl reasoned. "It's just that good friends don't always make good roommates."

Joe lived in a bachelor flat just a few miles from the campus and he offered his floor until I could locate my own place. But it wasn't easy to find lodging in that resort beach area, especially in the summer. When Joe's landlady discovered he was sharing his small quarters, she was upset. We explained the situation, promising I would be out as soon as I could locate a place. She tried to be understanding but made it clear that I could not stay much longer.

I was getting desperate looking for a place when one afternoon, while answering an ad, it seemed I had found the perfect deal. It was clean, the rent was fair, and the location was perfect, just a block from Joe's. The man with whom I was to share the apartment seemed witty and intelligent as we talked about the room I would have and my privileges in his home if I rented. I would have access to the kitchen, my own half of the refrigerator, certain cabinets for my things, and a pretty full run of the large apartment.

The man's name was Scott. He lived alone and had impeccable taste in interior decorating. There were dozens of ornate pictures and frames arranged artistically on the white Spanish walls. Potted plants grew in every nook and cranny, and in front of the large arched window overlooking Belmont Shores, stood a bust of Hermes. I was beginning to relax as we chatted about my summer classes at the college and his teaching position with handicapped children. It was the conspicuous bust of Hermes that gave me the courage to change the subject.

"I'm not a gay," I said as matter-of-factly as I could. "Oh, I'm not either," he replied. He was sitting across the room in a casual chair. "I do have a few gay friends who come by sometimes. I hope that wouldn't bother you. They are just some old friends of my wife and mine." He could see I was confused. "I'm divorced. We have two boys who live with their mother."

"Oh? How old are they?" I asked, trying to make conversation.

"Nine and seven," he smiled, "You'll meet them if you take the room, they come over regularly. Even their mother comes out sometimes to visit. We still get along pretty well."

Finally I was ready to get going. I had decided to rent the room and share the apartment with him. As I rose to my feet he began, "I guess I'd better tell you. Since you are going to move in, I mean." He paused as if searching for the right words. I sat back down.

He smiled sort of apologetically, "I am gay."

I didn't know what would be a suitable reply, so I just nodded.

"I hope you still want the room." He continued, "I promise I am not interested in you personally, I just think you would make a good renter. A guy has to be careful who he shares a place with these days."

I was sick. Joe's landlady was getting more upset every day. This guy seemed nice enough. A teacher for handicapped children and everything. I had been looking for two solid weeks and nothing. I was desperate.

"Well," I said before I had time to change my mind, "I don't guess it matters. I just want you to know I'm not interested in that sort of thing."

"Of course," he smiled engagingly. "I understand perfectly. I'm really not a HOMO-sexual, you know, I've been married. I just go out with men as well as women."

I was wondering what his wife thought about it when he added, "I promise to keep to myself where you're concerned."

Scott was as good for his word. During the month I lived there he never approached me in any way. In fact, after I got to

20

know him a little better, I found it interesting to discuss the gay issue which was at that time far underground, socially.

The fall term was about to begin when Joe and I rented a place down in Seal Beach. We were a little farther from school, but we both liked to body-surf and the advantages far out-weighed the disadvantages.

School was something I loved and hated at the same time. I hated the pressure of competition in my art classes, but I loved art and the atmosphere around the art buildings. Most of the time I was like one of the happy dogs that ran without leashes over the sunny college lawns. I was strong and healthy, tan of cheek and bare of foot. Life was all fresh sea air and warm vitality. I was meeting a lot of new people and finding that most of those in the art curriculum were like myself. There were some good artists who were really into their craft, but most of the people I knew were really into their dope.

I had been writing poetry since I was eighteen, a sort of diary. Today, as I read back through those pages written in the shade of the beautiful campus trees, I note a clot of blackness in the heart of the poet. Sometimes it seemed my very soul and body would be torn apart. I was in awful confusion. One day the birds would be singing and the sun shining down through the windows of heaven, the next day clouds of dark despair would clog my brain and everything I touched smelled of death. In my memory I recall the sunshine, the sandy beaches and the crystalline winds; but when I read back through that diary, I find bewilderment, thunder, and dark, hellish nights.

> a stark silhouette on a naked plain
> wondering about life
> a stark silhouette on a naked plain
> wondering about God
> a stark silhouette on a naked plain
> weeping

§§§

> and it was just another day
> anyone could have just held me in their arms

21

and my sickness would have gone
why am I so all alone
won't someone come and fill my heart

§§§

you speak of life
there's nothing to it
simply running
from one state to another
state of mind
state of health
state your full name
date of birth
rate of death
plan a transplant
one extra minute
one extra breath
and bury yourself
in business
and bury yourself
in fame
and state your full name
and bury yourself.

§§§

as I stand looking out to sea
my feet washed by the surf
I feel a need to be cleansed
a need for new enthusiasm
but as clogged as I am
it is only death that will take all the weight
away
someday I shall die
soon I hope
when on the beach I shall stand
and watch the sea reach through my feet
someday God will take me

I'm ready for your judgment
ready to confess
I've thrown all that you have given
to the wind or something less
so take me now
later finds me gone
I know my time is come
my truths are down to one

§§§

One evening an old friend of Joe's dropped in. His name was Tom, and from that first meeting it was apparent that we were vastly compatible in our outlooks on life. We stayed awake until three that morning discussing physical relativity (about which neither of us knew a thing). The subject was not as important, as our philosophies that tied us together. He had taken LSD once and wanted me to take his next "trip" with him. I was more than a little apprehensive about the subject as I had always told myself that just because I smoked marijuana, didn't mean I would ever go on to harder drugs. In those days, the talk of damaged chromosomes and mutated genetics was powerful. But Tom was so levelheaded and such a deep thinker; he practiced transcendental meditation, made top grades in school, and seemed to be a very sound person.

It was February twenty-second, a beautiful California spring day, when I rang his phone, "Hey, Tom, what are you doing today?"

His reply didn't bless my appetite for my first acid trip, "I was planning to study for a test on Monday. Why, what are you doing?"

"Oh, I just thought it would be a good day to take that acid trip. I just felt like this was the day for me."

"Look, why don't you come over?" he perked. "I've got it here, and maybe I can figure some way around my studies."

It had rained all the previous night. I was driving my Austin Healy 3000 with the top down. The air was rich and balmy as the sun played hide-and-seek behind the heavy little morning clouds. I swished down Seventh Street, tropical air fresh in my face.

The clouds were moving away from a large blue swath on

the horizon and I was sure we were in for one of those super sunny, cold, off-shore days. My bare foot danced on the clutch as I shifted down the gears and splashed through the gutter in front of Tom's apartment.

As I swallowed my first tablet of strawberry mescaline, my heart beat like a rookie astronaut. I was so excited and afraid of the territory I was entering that I made Tom drive the car as we started back to Seal Beach. By the time we entered my little apartment, my heart and lungs felt like one huge organ. We left the door open and soon the stuffy, sleepy air of Friday night was washed away by the breezes of a clear, wet Saturday morning.

I was breath-taken by the exquisite colors and hallucinations of the first two hours of my trip. How unbelievable to lie there on my back and watch giant neon-pink numbers sail across the ceiling. It was as though I had been seeing these things all my life and never before perceived them; this was not a foreign territory at all, but a fourth dimension of the same world I had lived in all my life. The walls were breathing; my Oriental rug was floating around like a raft on a shimmering sea. Our "fine art originals" in homemade frames were prancing up and down the walls like fluttering leaves in a gentle wind. Salty air filled my whole abdomen when I breathed, and everything I touched yielded before my throbbing hands. The sky was a glorious display of rainbows and lightning bolts. The whole universe was within reach. Fireworks exploded around the edges of my peripheral vision.

I found psychedelic drugs very beautiful to look upon. Satan does not use ugly things to entrap us. When David saw Bathsheba washing herself the Bible tells us that she was very beautiful to look upon. If the letters L-S-D abbreviated the chemicals used in these drugs, they may also stand for the power behind such subversion; Lucifer, Satan, Devil.

In my first month of acid tripping everything I thought, did, and believed was again modified. I was absolutely positive that through this medium I would find the path to God. We called them "mind-expanding" drugs. I thought I was expanding my mind to God as I filled my system with lies, poison, and insanity. Before that summer ever burned its mark into the sands of the Pacific Southwest, my mind had been branded by the tracks of departing

24

reality. I was becoming a foggy-headed, simple-minded doper. I wouldn't have believed it though; I thought I was a deeply perceptive super-sensitive, ancient philosopher.

One evening while in the psychedelic dimension, I was lying on my back, visually fixing on a "Jefferson Airplane" poster we had tacked to the ceiling. Driving, screaming "acid rock" was catapulting out of the stereo system. Through meditation, I was trying to believe I could absorb into the atmosphere and reappear in far-away San Francisco. But it just wasn't happening. And then I was interrupted by Joe sticking his head between me and the poster. After we exchanged remarks, I started to drift off into the music again when I was startled by a strange phenomenon. Out from under the stereo turntable a liquid was running like a little river filling the fissures of the carpet. It was grey-brown in color and was composed of millions of dead faces. The effect it had on me was liquid Death. Each face, like a tiny seed, had its own unique expression. I looked around the room for repose, but on every surface and on every different texture were those faces. The appalling stuff was rubbery to the touch and seemed to grip my flesh with suckers. Bones and teeth and nostrils were gouging, biting, and sucking. In a terror, I ran barefooted out of the apartment, down the steps and into the street. The waves of the Pacific were crashing along the shore just across the alley in the darkness, and I ran to the water hoping to find rest from my morbid hallucination.

There was no depth in space. Stars clung to the air above me. The apartment buildings along the beach ran together in a mass of paper-like paste-ups. The icy water washed around my ankles as I stood in the sand looking out toward the horizon which was not miles away as usual, but right there, inches from my nose. Logic had run away. I plunged into the surf, trying to escape life itself. When I surfaced, the water seemed to cling to me like honey. The air was so thick I could hardly breathe it down. I dived into an oncoming breaker; I knew it was time for me to die.

Joe perceived my peril and dove in. He couldn't see me, but in a desperate quest he located me beneath the surface and dragged me up to safety. I came to, sneezing and coughing saltwater onto the warm sand. The horror had left me. I lay there on the beach, panting.

I tried to stay away from acid for a while, but before a fortnight, I was again in its paralyzing grip. Death had become an obsession. I was desperate to find God and leave the pressures of this world.

I've given up
given in
given out
but given to no one
where is peace
where is love
where am I
where is one thing worth living for
the reason the answer the truth I want so much
where is the spirit hiding

§§§

I have nothing
but the wind blows
nothing still the grass grows
pray for death
the sun shines
dream of peace and watch the death crawl
live for death and feel a child fall

spinning walls and screaming calls
and darkness
screaming needles of death
float bodiless through space
turn and cry into the sun
scream to God and cling
HELP ME FATHER

join the souls spread like fans
across the universe
spread holy arms and feel existence
spread me like forever past the stars
past the light past the end

stretch me from the corners of Your existence
poke me into the textures of Your being
let me melt through You forever.

§§§

It was almost midnight one warm spring evening in 1969. I was sitting behind one of the large drafting tables in the Graphic Design Building in a feverish attempt to complete a monumental project that was due the next morning. I was in my last year of college, graduation lay just around the corner, but I could not face the work that lay before me on the table. I had messed around and put it off until it had become impossible to complete. I was no longer able to cope with the responsibilities of higher education. I knew it was no use trying to make it through to the end of the year, I was too far behind in all my classes. There at that drawing table I came out of my drug-imposed day-dream and smacked into reality. I felt sick. In the morning there would be sober business going on in the graphic design department, but I would not be there.

The next week I officially dropped all my classes. I knew I would have to go home and face my parents, but I put it off as long as possible, finally showing up on the pretense of a weekend visit. I tried to find the right time and the right way to tell them, but how could it ever be easy? They had sacrificed to finance my way through college, and now in the last year, I was quitting with no real reason.

It was not but a few days until Mom had dragged it out of me that I was on drugs. You might as well have told her I was a hopelessly crippled and mentally disabled. That very day she called the county hospital and made an appointment for me to see a clinical psychologist.

Doctor Freidman was a young man, under forty, very congenial and understanding. He asked why I was there.

"Well," I really didn't know how to start. I was ready for him to tell me why I was there. "My mother found out I've been taking drugs," I said. "She thought I ought to see a doctor or something."

"How did she find out you were on drugs?"

"She's been on me for months to assure her I wasn't taking anything," I said.

"Finally she just asked me too many times and I told her."

"What drugs have you taken?" he asked.

"Mostly marijuana," I said. "I've taken some LSD, too."

"Apparently your mother thinks these things are dangerous. How do you feel about it?"

"Well, I don't know." But then I had to admit, "Yeah. I guess they are a little dangerous."

Doctor Freidman never did intimate whether he thought they were dangerous or not. In fact, he never said much of anything except to keep the conversation going. I began to feel safe confiding in him; he seemed to be genuinely concerned about me, and I knew he would not turn me over to the law. It felt good to open up to a conventional person about my life, and after about forty-five minutes he had somehow extracted quite a lot of my history.

"The greatest mistake you made," concluded the good doctor, "was that you told your mother."

I guess I looked a little confused. "It's like this," he explained. "You love your mother, right?"

"Yeah."

"Well, then to tell her a lie because you love her and don't want to hurt her is really like telling the truth." He smiled, "If you had continued to tell her that you didn't take drugs, it would have been the truth because it would have been out of love. You would have saved her all this anxiety."

"Oh," I said.

I saw Doctor Freidman regularly right on through the summer. It made me feel good to confide in someone about my secrets. My visits made it easier to deal with my parents. I kept on living as I wanted to, lying to keep peace in the home, and then the doctor would teach me not to feel so guilty about it.

§§§

Monty and I worked together in a clothing store in Bakersfield. He had a lot of friends in town, most of them dopers,

28

and I wanted to get to know them. My old friends from Bakersfield had either gone off to other places, or had settled down with families and careers and were now out of my sphere of society.

Monty was learning to play the bass guitar, and he and his friends were going to have a jam session. I took some LSD with them and we all settled down for some hard rock. I had taken so much acid by this time that it was second nature. Everything was bouncing off everything else. Pieces of the wall were bolting into the room. Pieces of the chair were reflecting off the couch. The sound was terrific, pushing the air in front of it in waves. The corners of the ceiling were turning inside-out, stretching toward the center of the room and reflect back into space. My body felt like it was stitched to the air with electric thread and a million rainbows ran back and forth across the sky outside the open door.

All of a sudden I couldn't breathe and started to lose consciousness. I strained to keep aware of my surroundings. The music was taking my breath. Monty looked like another person. One of the guys' wives came out of the kitchen and offered me a coke. A siege of paranoia struck and I imagined they were all out to get me. I didn't know any of them, not even Monty really.

I stepped outside to try to get hold of myself. The afternoon was hot and dry as only Bakersfield could make it. The driveway burned my bare feet, but it felt good, reminding me of days when I was a kid playing in the yard.

I had not been outside very long when Monty and a couple of the guys came out for a break. They were standing around on the grass and sitting on the curb. It was scaring me to death for them just to be there talking and smoking. I started down the street and Monty followed after me.

I sat down on the sidewalk in front of a vacant lot.

Sensing there was something wrong, Monty sat down and tried to comfort me a little. "Just hang on, Brad," he said. "You know acid's just a temporary insanity."

"I know," I answered, "but I can't keep my head together." Acid may have been a temporary insanity to him, but to me it was becoming less temporary all the time. The breaking point between the rational and irrational was always very near. I was about to come unglued.

"Come back in and relax," Monty smiled reassuringly.

"You'll feel better in a few minutes." He walked back over to the house and disappeared around the corner of the garage.

I sat there trying to figure out what to do and finally started down the street in the opposite direction. I was only a mile or so from my old junior high school and from there it was easy to make the next couple of miles home. I was sure I could make it before dark, and besides the familiar streets were well lighted. It never occurred to me that I left my Austin Healy sitting in the driveway of Monty's friend's house.

As I walked briskly along, the sidewalk seemed to bite into my bare feet. Then I noticed that the old stream of dead faces was filling the cracks in the sidewalk. They were biting me. I stepped up my pace trying not to think about it. Soon the faces covered the street in a solid sheet. On every rock and pebble was a perfect little face like a detailed carving. But they were not carvings, they were real people, dead people. The road ran through the foothills of the Sierra Nevada Mountains along the eastern sides of Bakersfield. Where the road cut through the hills, the rocks and clods looked out at me. The entire cosmos was cursed with a horrible spell. Some of the faces were as large as life and as detailed as any clay mask I had seen in my college art days: eyelashes, nostrils, teeth, frowns, grimaces, pain, death.

When I opened the front door of my parents' apartment, the cat took one look at me and disappeared like lightning into the back bedroom. There was a note lying on the dining table. I thought I would lose my mind completely. I picked up the phone and dialed the number of the family where my parents were having supper, and the receiver grabbed my hand like a hot octopus tentacle, its acidic suckers burning my flesh.

"Hello, is my mom there?"

"Oh, hi, Brad. Just a minute."

"Hello."

"Hello, Mom."

"Hello, Honey. You got my note?" she asked cheerfully.

"Yes," I labored. There was an uncomfortable pause.

"Is there something wrong, Brad?"

"Yes."

"Well, Honey, what is it?"

Another long pause. "I love you," was all I could manage.

"Do you want us to come home?"

"Yes." I hung up. The yellow receiver looked perfectly normal as it sucked against my burning hand.

I was sitting cross-legged in one of the big living room chairs when Mom and Dad came through the door. The cat came sneaking out of the back of the apartment, its hair looked like it had been painted on with a stick, now this way and now that.

My mother was manifestly anxious, "What is it, Brad?"

"I'm having a bad trip."

She looked like she thought I was dying. "What can we do?" she asked kindly.

"Just be nice to me," I said. "I'll probably be all right."

But instead of getting better, I got worse. All night I tossed in fits on the sofa and did not sleep at all. Monday morning Mom called our old family doctor and he prescribed black and green tranquilizers which I took all day; but nothing changed much except that my hallucinations went deeper into my psychic regions. For a while I thought I was in heaven and my dad was God. In one fit of confusion I locked myself in the bathroom and studied if it might be possible to flush myself down the commode. I imagined I could come up in the Seal Beach surf again, and out of the bad trip.

Tuesday morning, after pushing eggs and bacon around on my plate, I fell into a dark mental whirlpool. I curled up in a ball on my bed in the den, shut my eyes, and denied existence itself. I can still remember sailing out through my consciousness like through the upper end of a tornado. When I sailed past the last bits of thought and memory, the terrain was that of an outer darkness. Sanity had been left far behind in the storm and I flew out into a black empty space. For a few moments, I was all alone out there. Then in the distance I could see something approaching. It was simply three capital letters: G-O-D.

That afternoon Doctor Freidman admitted me into the psychiatric ward at Kern General Hospital. What I went through during those next forty-eight hours could never be described in the human tongue. I was locked in an empty room with a bed in the middle and heavy wire mesh on the windows. The walls had fist marks in them, but I did not realize it at first, I thought they were eyes. I thought I had left the surface of the earth and was down in its center, and those were people looking in at me. The eyes were clear and watery and absolutely real. The light in the ceiling chattered and blinked, but I could not understand what it was saying. To use the word "terrified" comes far short of describing what was going on inside me. Fears, anxieties and hallucinations swarmed my mind until the doctors gave my parents the hope of a fifty-fifty chance that I would ever recover to mental health.

The mind-crushing details and monumental fears of the first twenty-four hours finally gave way under medication to a state of silent paranoia. The third day found me in prayer to the God of heaven, the same God who had written His name on the last dark sky of my right mind.

I asked Mom for a Bible and she brought me an ancient thing that had been my dad's when he was a child. I read some but could not make much sense out of it. There were colorful pictures every so often and just looking at them gave me some peace.

God brought me back from the regions of mania and answered the sometimes audible prayers that went up out of that hospital from the soul of a terrified child. And God was the single reality upon which I re-built my sanity through the next weeks of my life.

Chapter Three

DRAFT DODGER

During the month that followed my stay in the psych ward, I worked hard at selling my Austin Healy and preparing to move to Toronto, Ontario. Every young man my age who was not in college could expect to be drafted immediately as the war in Viet Nam was at its peak.

I chose Toronto in dodging the draft rather than any other Canadian city because while living in Seal Beach I had been introduced to a Canadian girl who had won my undivided attention. After Jill and I met, she had extended her California vacation indefinitely. Then when I quit school, she flew back to her home in Toronto

I made my move in July, 1969. By that time there was a special counseling and job-finding service in most major Canadian cities, created specifically by and for American draft dodgers just like me. With their help it was not long before I had a job making submarine sandwiches and was heading for Niagara Falls to "re-cross" the border with all the red tape necessary for immigration. Since I had not received my induction notice back home, the United States Government was not looking for me; so after only two hours in the Canadian Immigration office, I was legally classified a "Landed Immigrant."

Even though Toronto was not far from the States, there was a definite foreignness about the city. The subways were alien with their electric smells and sounds; so were the many olive-skinned people with European accents and the strange brands of magazines and cigarettes. I strained hard to savor it as the life of a poet, but I felt like an oddball. I lived so far from Jill that I rarely got to see her. I tried to fit in with the "freaks" in Yorkville and ended up lonely and miserable.

A few blocks from the city center I had rented a sleazy two-room flat in an old, grey section of Toronto, back behind the skyscrapers. I had to share a common bathroom on the second floor with a black woman and the transient inhabitants of a communal crash pad. There was a sink just outside my door for the use of the whole second floor, and a messy refrigerator where I kept my free submarine sandwiches and chocolate milk.

Jim, one of the guys I worked with at Mr. Submarine, invited me home one night for a little marijuana and supper. He was a deserter from the U. S. Army. Jim and his wife and little boy lived in a small apartment with a picnic table and packing crates for furniture. His dream was to save enough money to buy a piece of land and start a commune. In the meantime, he had to be satisfied with painting trees, shrubs, mountains and clouds all around his walls and ceiling. The effect was supposed to be dramatic as you sat there at the picnic table, but I remember more clearly the garbage on the kitchen floor, the stink, and the dim, dismal sadness that hung in the air with our smoke. After bland spaghetti, false philosophy, and dreams of a commune where everybody would do his own thing, they drove me down to the old brick building I was trying to call home.

When they drove off I remained on the sidewalk for a long time wondering what I was doing there. Toronto? An immigrant? A foreigner? If I had been in France, I could not have felt farther from home. The front door was unlocked and a yellow night-light was all that graced the foyer of the old boarding house. I made my way up the creaking stairway which landed on a wide hall on the second floor. The linoleum was worn to the boards down the middle of the hall where a thousand homeless, aimless losers like myself had dragged their dusty feet.

I wasn't dusty. Life was brimming in me. I was twenty-two, young and strong. But there was a certain weariness enshrouding me — the weariness a loser feels deep down in his heart no matter how young he is, a despair known only to those who have stuck someone else's key in someone else's door and have fallen down across someone else's bed and stared at his own personal stuff lying around on someone else's floor. Ragged curtains. Dust. Other people's dust. And strange odors drifting about, left from other days.

I kicked off my clothes and crawled under the blanket I had borrowed from the landlady. All was silent except for the dripping of the tap in the sink outside my room. The hall light was always on, throwing its yellow reflection under my door. I thought about pushing a towel up to it, but was too shot to put my bare foot to that cold floor again.

It was a funny little room, a kind of a doll-house with high ceilings. Above the regular window was a stained glass window with wooden scrollwork around it. As I lay there on my side, the streetlight through the stained glass gave the impression that someone's big face was peaking in. The giant was looking for me, I pretended. I stayed perfectly still for I knew any movement would give me away and he would break down the house and get me. At the time I did not give it much thought, but since then I have wondered, maybe the giant was reality.

§§§

I had been in Toronto about three months when I gave in to the pangs of homesickness. Since I still had not received my draft notice back home, I decided to return for a visit. This could be my last chance to go back to the States a free man.

Paramahansa Yogananda's autobiography lay in my lap as I sat staring out the window of the American Airlines DC-10 which was carrying me back across the continent toward Los Angeles International. The captain broke the silence by pointing out Denver far to the right. Miles below, the great prairie met the Rocky Mountains in a dynamic clash; the whole earth leaped up from its flat, dull, grey existence into a vertical purple mural. Granite cathedrals cast shadows as large as whole ranches out onto the plain. Now as far as the eye could see, the earth was crumpled and pleated. Snow and clouds took turns trying to hide the great mountain peaks as we flew.

Next came the Badlands of Utah, home of rattlesnakes and lizards. Then there was the red desert of Arizona; through that desert the Colorado River grinds eternally around the buttes and ravines at the bottom of the Grand Canyon. From my window in the sky it looked like the sun had come too close to this spot. Sparse pine woods were black against the dry earth. Lacy fjords of dead desert reached up into the high red mesas, while tiny ribbon rivers found each other out on the flatlands.

Before I knew it, we were passing over Indio. On the northern horizon I could see the blue haze of the Mojave Desert. Homesickness was giving way to a richness in my breast. As we crossed the range that separates Palm Springs and the Los Angeles

35

basin, I could see the exhaust of a zillion cars pouring like soup over the brim of the mountain and rolling off into the high solitude of the Mojave. The Los Angeles basin was full, a brown ocean of fumes.

Freeways, like blood vessels, pumped an endless stream of traffic to and from ten million destinations. I felt at home. This was California. I slipped Paramahansa Yogananda down into my satchel as the backyards, swimming pools, mailmen, and street signs raced under the descending jet.

We flew over Interstate 405 so low I could tell the make of every car, and with a shudder and a yelp we were on the runway. Engines whined to a high pitch. It was like slowing a flood — the ring of turbines, the hissing of unsealed vacuums. Now the crackling of microphones and loud speakers. People were buzzing excitedly; crowds craning, smiling, crying. There's my Mom. She's happy to see me. Dad stands there shyly as Mom hugs me and kisses red lipstick on my face. She is crying. I am her draft-dodger son, a dope head — she loves me. Dad shakes my hand. Through the din of loud-speakers and chatter, we make our way to the baggage-claim area.

I had not been gone that long, but sitting in my dad's car watching the familiar countryside brought real comfort. Even dry old Bakersfield was comforting. That rat-hole down in Toronto had taken its toll on me. I was glad to be home. Mom had her Mexican spaghetti ready shortly after we came through the door. She had prepared it especially for the occasion, it was my favorite.

§§§

When I tried to phone Joe in Seal Beach, I found he had moved from our old apartment. I finally got his mother and she told me he was in Long Beach living in a house with Paul and Shelby.

Paul answered the phone and said Joe was working that night. I told him I was back in the States and wanted to come see them for a couple of weeks while I was in California. I did not know how much room they had and wondered if it would be inconvenient.

Joe had known Paul and Shelby for years, and while I lived

with him back in college days I had gotten to know them quite well. Paul was one of the best artists at Long Beach State; by now he was ready for his Bachelor's in Fine Arts. Shelby was his plump little wife who had a way of mothering those of us who were not quite so settled. Little Paul junior was about three.

Paul said they had a huge house; in fact Bob, another friend, was living in one of the downstairs rooms. Paul was sure everyone would be glad to have me come for as long as I liked.

"Tell Joe I'll probably be there about one or two tomorrow afternoon," I said.

It was a huge, white, two-storey house that looked like something a wealthy old couple might have on some high and windy cliff over the shores of Waikiki. It sat on the corner of a fairly busy street, but had palm trees towering all around. Thick shrubs garnished the little yards, and a wide covered porch ran along the two sides of the house facing the streets. On top of the porch was a second floor veranda. The thing looked like a mansion.

I found the place deserted and the doors locked, but through the front window I could see Paul's painting of the 'Motorcycle Man' and I knew it was the house. I had been sitting on the huge shady porch about half an hour when Joe came around the corner. There was my old friend smiling brightly with a cigarette in the corner of his mouth.

Greeting him with an exaggerated tone, I snorted, "I tried to find a way up to the veranda! Wow! how did you guys ever find this monster?"

"Shelby found it in the paper last month." Joe tilted his head so the smoke would not get in his eyes as he unlocked the multi-windowed front door. "Come on up while I get rid of this stuff," he said with hearty grin, "and I'll show you how to get to the veranda."

"It's a good thing Paul's 'Motorcycle Man' is on the wall," I said, "I wasn't sure I was even at the right house till I looked in the window."

He led me up to the second storey. "This is my room," he said as he dumped his books and art satchel on the bed. "Right out here is the door to the veranda. Paul and Shel's room has an outside door, too." We went out and around the corner of the house. The sunshine was almost blinding against the white siding. A gentle evening breeze was beginning to blow in from the ocean which was just at the end of the street.

What I told Joe of my stay in Canada was all pretty romantic and adventurous sounding. I did not think it necessary to describe the loneliness and despair. I told him about the "Village" where all the hippies hung out, and how I had worked for Mr. Submarine and gotten free food. I even included Jim and his far-out apartment; I just left out the garbage and the sadness.

"Paul told me on the phone he wasn't sure if Bob would be staying with you much longer," I said. "What's he going to do?"

"Well, if you want to know the truth, I don't think he knows himself," Joe raised his eyebrows. "What do you mean?"

"Well," he said, "He and Paul had a kind of fight over finances the other day and I doubt that we'll see Bob around here much at all."

Bob was different, we had determined that long ago. I mean, he was always clean-cut; he was still true-blue to his old boyhood girlfriend, Cecilia, and he never would smoke dope with us. Then, of course, the previous year, when he had gone into training to be a cop, all our doubt had vanished. For sure, Bob was different.

"Yeah," Joe continued, "Paul loaned him fifty dollars rent when we moved in here last month. He was supposed to pay him back by last week, but you know Bob," he smiled. "He just can't seem to scrape the money together. Now Paul is wondering where next month's rent is going to come from and Bob is getting hard to locate. He hasn't slept here since Sunday."

Joe and I were still sitting on the front porch when Paul and Shelby arrived. I greeted them with a happy, "Hello!" and was surprised when it was met with only a quick smile from Paul as he strode into the house far ahead of his wife. When Shelby got to the porch her face was grave. "Paul just went by to see Bob and get his money," she breathed with her hand on the door knob. "'Just about got in a fight with Bob's father!"

Paul was sitting on the couch trying to get a pair of work boots on but was so mad he could not get the things laced up. "I'll kill him!" He was literally foaming at the mouth. Shelby sat by him and tried to calm him down and get him to stay home. Joe and

I had to chuckle, he was really having a hard time getting his boots laced up. "What happened?" Joe had to know more.

"Bob's dad kept putting Paul off about where Bob was," Shelby explained. "Finally Paul accused them both of being a couple of liars and cowards." Paul stopped lacing to listen. "Paul thinks Bob was right there in the house all the time. It did kind of look that way. Anyway, Bob's dad said he was going to call the police if we didn't leave. I thought Paul was going to hit him when. . ."

Paul interrupted in a shout, "He was standing there covering for his coward son!" He had given up on the boots and was sitting back on the couch trying to describe the scene in his own words, but the farther he got, the madder he got until he finally went back to the laces. He was huffing and puffing. The atmosphere was so electric that finally Joe started to laugh; then we all just crumbled in hilarity.

"Come on Paul, cool off for a while," Joe encouraged, "where do you think you're going anyway?"

"Back to that house. I know Bob was in there."

"So what," Joe reasoned. "It's not worth fighting over; you'll get your money back sooner or later. You know Bob wouldn't just keep it."

"Yeah, but.., well.., it's the principle of the thing. That coward! Why doesn't he just come out and face me and tell me what he's going to do instead of sending his old dad out there to head me off?" Paul was in earnest, "I've got a wife and a kid! He knows we don't have any money. And now we've got this big house and how are we going to pay for it all ourselves? He gave his word!"

I thought I might as well get into the debate at this point. It looked like a perfect opportunity. "Didn't I see a bunch of his stuff in that bedroom back there?"

"Yeah," Paul growled, "I guess he thinks he still lives here, but he's got another think coming."

"Well, he'll be back for his stuff, won't he? You don't have to go chasing him around the country," I said. "Just wait for him to show up and then lower the boom."

"Sure!" Paul returned bitterly. "And who is going to pay for next month's rent that's due right now?"

Shelby broke in, "Paul thinks Bob should not only pay what he owes us for last month's rent, but also for next month's rent whether he stays here or not." She did not sound convinced about the ethics of his reasoning.

"Absolutely!" Paul stood up, "It's only right to give a person thirty days' notice. That's the way it's done."

"But, Honey," she reasoned, "you're not the landlord."

"I don't care who's the landlord! I'm the guy who's going to have to foot the bill." Paul was angry. Standing in the middle of the room he raised his voice even higher as he pointed at the door, "He's the one who's not doing right!"

I was sure I had the financial solution in my pocket, but the electricity was snapping around until I did not know if I should open my mouth or not. Finally I broke in, "Listen, I've got an idea." All eyes fixed on me as if to say, "Where'd you come from?"

"Well," I said, "if you guys don't mind me living in Bob's room, I'll pay next month's rent."

It was as if the sun had just risen. We all looked instinctively at Paul. He looked at Shelby with a shrug and sat down. "Great." Then he smiled for the first time. "Throw Bob's junk in a box and put it in the hall closet upstairs. I'm going to get that money." He kicked his boots into the middle of the living room floor, "Let's eat, I'm starved. Hey, Brad, good to see you."

§§§

Staying in the "Big House" was like a sweet dream in my mixed-up life, the calm before the storm. What burst my fleecy bubble was a phone call from home one cool October evening.

"Hi, Mom. What are you doing?"

"Oh, not much really. Just thought I'd call and see how you were."

"I've been working in a bookstore downtown. Other than that I'm just having a good time." I always tried to sound secure and well fed to Mom. "You ought to see this house, Mom. It's really nice. Just like living at home almost."

"Well, I'm glad you're comfortable, Honey," she said warmly. We talked for a minute and then she put on a more serious

40

tone of voice. "I got some mail for you today."

"Oh," I said. My heart sank.

"I think it's your draft notice," she said. "It's from the United States Army Induction Center in Fresno. Do you want me to open it?"

"Yeah. See what it is."

"Just a minute," she rattled some papers. "Oh, it's for your physical examination. You're supposed to report to the bus station here in Bakersfield a week from this Thursday." Nobody was surprised, especially me. We all knew it was coming; and we knew that when it came, I would be heading for Toronto. It was all arranged. Mr. Submarine even had a job waiting for me.

Joe, Paul and Shelby were sweet and sympathetic which was comforting. But then they began in unison to persuade me to go into the army and serve my time. Of course, my mother and father were all for me going into the army so I could remain an American citizen with the freedom and privileges involved. No doubt they would have been much prouder of their son if he had the courage and character to serve his country. I knew it was tearing them apart to see me leave. But when my nearest friends started in on me, I was devastated. I had spent all my life hardening my heart against my parents' wishes. But these people were different, they were my peers, my world.

I guess my stay in the Big House had influenced me too much. It had been too comfortable, too sweet, too free. Somehow it had become a symbol of America. How could I just walk out and leave forever my friends, my Pacific Ocean, my California, my Mom and Dad? When I thought about Toronto, all I could see were those two sleazy rooms and that cold, hard, half-eaten submarine sandwich in the common refrigerator. The security of home and the affection of loved ones suddenly became more powerful than the irresponsible, rebellious, and childish self that generally reigned in my life.

Chapter Four

YOU'LL NEVER MAKE A SOLDIER

Standing in shorts and tee shirt on a cold concrete floor along with eighty-five other guys, looking over the papers I was carrying to Station B, I found myself burning on the inside. How did I ever get talked into this? What am I doing here? I ought to be in Canada, free.

Files, interviews, urine samples, examinations of every type imaginable. Standing silently in long lines with grave young men answering cold objective questions. I was almost sure the letter from Doctor Freidman and my record of being in the psych ward would keep me out of the army. It didn't. Neither did my confession and written statement to having taken various and sundry drugs. My high-arched feet came closer to keeping me out than anything else, but finally the second doctor was called in to take a look at them. I was signed, sealed, stamped, and delivered "qualified for active duty."

In a small carpeted room with wood paneling and a huge American flag standing beside a sort of pulpit, about forty of us crowded together and took the oath. I raised my right hand and repeated after the man in uniform standing behind the rostrum. He had scrambled eggs all over his hat and ribbons hanging down the front of his coat. He believed in what he was saying; he was almost enthusiastic. I felt a million miles away.

§§§

It was about 10:00 p.m. The Greyhound pulled up to a guard booth in the middle of nowhere. A floodlight illuminated the entrance and a soldier waved the bus to a stop.

"Here comes another load of turkeys," the guard chuckled to himself as he approached the bus door. "I wish they'd let me cut their hair the first time." He actually grinned as he took the sheet of papers from the driver. Then he waved the bus on, his helmet shining under the light. We rolled into the darkness, leaving him standing at the gate which separated two tall chain-link fences that ran in opposite directions away from the guard shack.

It was a fifteen minute ride from the fence through a dark oak forest. Soon we were heading down a well-lighted street with barracks on either side. Finally, we pulled up in front of a two-storey frame building. The bus door hissed open and we were ordered to disembark. "LINE UP IN FRONT OF THE BARRACKS FACING ME!" shouted a Negro sergeant. He was wearing a black helmet with a wide chrome stripe around it. The bus drove off. He was inserting papers into a clipboard. Then he looked up. We did not know whether to stand at attention or what. Most of us were in jeans and sport-shirts and had hair well over our ears; some had it down their backs. It was 10:30 at night and the black sergeant had on sun glasses.

"ANDERSON, EUGENE. . ." He looked up from his clipboard.

"Here"

The bus had never stopped for water; we were all there. "THIS WILL BE YOUR HOME FOR THE NEXT FEW DAYS! FILE UPSTAIRS, FIND A BUNK AND GET IN BED BY ELEVEN O'CLOCK! LIGHTS GO OUT AT ELEVEN!"

I was on the top bunk in the center of the large barrack. There must have been fifty of us in there and everyone was a stranger to me. I could not sleep. Others were snoring restfully, but my heart was hammering like a wild animal in a trap. Out the window I could see the floodlights down the street revealing the roofs of other barracks. I lay there all night without sleep and made up my mind that I would get out of the army whatever the cost.

At 4:00 a.m. I decided to get a shower and shave before the rush. Five toilets sat along one wall of the large latrine; I guessed the lack of privacy was to promote a kind of conference or powwow atmosphere.

Before the stars began to fade, we were lined up and headed for breakfast. The next three days were spent in the receiving station getting our hair cut off, going through orientation, getting our fatigues and other army paraphernalia. They gave each of us a cardboard box and told us to send all our civilian clothes home. I kept a pair of jeans and a green tee shirt in my laundry bag; I was going to need something to wear when I got out.

They treated us rather mean around the receiving station, but it did not bother me too much. Some of it I even found

43

amusing. They taught us how to brush our teeth, which took a solid hour of detailed instruction. They taught us how to take a shower, which body parts to wash first, which last, and how to rinse off. We learned how to keep our razors clean and soap dry, and just a lot of things a creature from outer space would need to know upon his arrival to earth. I thought this was all ridiculous until I better got to know some of the creatures they were training.

We left the receiving station in a drab green bus. I was sitting in the seat that ran across the back end. After a five minute ride, we pulled up in the shade of a gigantic concrete building. This was to be my home for the next eight weeks of basic training. There was a sergeant in a Smokey Bear hat standing at the door of the bus screaming like a mad man. My duffel bag weighed about seventy-five pounds and was impossible to get between the seats. My heart was thundering as I tried to hoist it up and over, making my way haltingly to the front where the sergeant was throwing a tremendous fit. His face was bright red with anger and he was yelling at the top of his lungs when I came down the steps, "HURRY! HURRY! HURRY!" I was so humiliated and intimidated, I thought I was going to faint. I could not lift my duffel bag another inch. It was bouncing along the blacktop. The man in the Smokey Bear hat was outraged. I thought he was going to hit me, "HURRY! HURRY! YOU SHOULD HAVE BEEN THERE BY NOW!!" I was straining. His voice was like a lion's roar, "YOU'LL NEVER MAKE A SOLDIER!"

I could have told him that.

§§§

I had not been to church in years. That first Sunday in basic, I went to church. Not that I had to go or even that I could not have found anything else to do, church just seemed the place to go after the week I had put in.

That evening I was leaning on the window ledge of our third floor barracks looking across Monterey Bay and into the darkness. I could see the lights of another city many miles to the north reflecting off the Pacific.

"Hey, Ray," I addressed my bunk mate, "do you know what town that is across the bay?"

The fact that Ray and I shared the same bed frame (he on the bottom bunk and I on the top) was not the greatest factor in causing our friendship. Although he lived right under me and our foot lockers were back to back, it was obvious from the start that this six-foot-three, red-haired trainee and I had a lot in common in our former civilian lifestyle and attitudes.

He looked out the window. Far across the Bay the little city was twinkling. "Way over there?" he pointed. "That's Santa Cruz. You've never been there?"

"No," I said, "but I wish I was there now, free to go as I please."

On that November night in 1969, little did I know what a big part the town of Santa Cruz would eventually play in my life. As I drifted off to sleep on my top bunk, just across the bay in the Santa Cruz hills there was series of evangelistic meetings in progress in a certain campground tabernacle. Something spiritual was happening in Santa Cruz. It was not the great Welsh revival by any means, but God was moving in a sovereign way through a group of people who would someday be among my dearest loved ones.

§§§

"YOU PEOPLE CAN DO THESE THINGS I TELL YOU TO DO!" It was Senior Drill Sergeant Duanas in his broken English. Senior Drill was a Hawaiian; barely five feet tall, he stood like a little brick fort. He was made of metal from the inside out and had the wonderful ability to make us hate him and love him at the same time. He was standing on a wooden platform that put him five feet above the trainees. In a white tee shirt, his legs spread to shoulder width, he was holding his stout brown arms straight out from the shoulders, making little circles with his fingertips. My shoulders were burning with fatigue as my "wings" circled round and round. I knew it was only a matter of seconds before they would collapse.

The other drill sergeants were walking up and down the P. T. field making sure we were keeping up with Sergeant Duanas. Finally, he let us put our arms down. Sighs of relief came from all over the field.

"YOU ALL A BUNCH OF WOMEN!" He jumped down in front of the company and strode briskly down the line until he was facing a blond kid who was a bit overweight and obviously angry with the workout.

"YOU!" Senior Drill shouted in his face, "ON YOUR BELLY!"

Down he went as we all looked on.

"ON YOUR BACK, BIG BOY!" There was something funny about it and there was something not funny. "ON YOUR BELLY!"

"ON YOUR BACK!" Sand was on the side of his red sweating face.

"ON YOUR BELLY. . . . . ON YOUR BACK. . . . ." Sergeant Duanas strode back to the platform. The blond boy was still on his back, as with one leap Senior Drill pulled himself up on the stand. "EVERYBODY, ON YOUR BACK!"

Two minutes later there wasn't anything funny in the whole world.

Finally we were putting on our shirts, it was almost time for lunch. Before half of us could get our shirts tucked in, Senior Drill was jogging down the row looking as crisp as a morning breeze, "YOU PEOPLE BETTER MOVE!"

They were already forming up in ranks when I scrambled into position. "QUICKLY! QUICKLY!"

As we marched off the P. T. field, Senior Drill Duanas was calling the cadence, "YOUR LEF. . . YOUR LEF. . . YOUR LEF, RIGHT, LEF . . . I GOT A GAL LIVES OVER THE HILL. . . ." As the company gave the repeat, something akin to joy went up my back — a thrill, a quickening. Senior Drill was marching alongside the company, almost two hundred men in perfect unison, every boot coming down at the same count. "IF SHE AIN'T LEFT SHE LIVES THERE STILL. . .YOUR LEF. . .YOUR LEF. . . DOUBLE-TIME . . . HO!"

We rounded the corner at a running cadence and headed up the street where I could see the huge concrete barracks standing in file. I was wheezing strongly, lungs burning in the cool ocean breeze. I doubted seriously that I could make it all the way up the hill.

"HIDEY HIDEY HIDEY HO. . . HIDEY HIDEY HIDEY

46

HO. . ." I could barely breathe, let alone sing. "IT'S THE FORT ORD BOOGY. . . WHAT A CRAZY SONG. . . ." Senior Drill was out in front running backward. He was grinning. "YOU PEOPLE CAN DO THESE THINGS I TELL YOU TO DO!" I knew I loved this little Hawaiian with the sweating face.

§§§

One balmy December night Ray and I were sitting out on the mess hall roof, which was easily accessible from our third floor barracks window. He had gotten hold of a little marijuana and we were enjoying the view of the Bay in the night. The lights of Monterey lay across to the southwest, and far to the north the twinkling lights of Santa Cruz reflected off the water.

As I have said, something spiritual was happening in Santa Cruz. Of course, as Ray and I sat smoking dope on the mess hall roof, I had no idea how powerfully those influences would one day affect my life. And since Santa Cruz, and certain people who lived there are so important to this story, let me introduce some of their history now

It all started in the mid 1960's when two boys answered an invitation to attend Sunday school not far from their home in the Santa Cruz mountains. They were Clifford and Christopher Walrath, sons of a businessman and his wife. As is the course of events in most churches, there came the time for the annual Christmas program. Mr. and Mrs. Walrath attended.

Some weeks later, "Wally" Walrath was puttering around his little farm when the preacher pulled up the steep driveway. Wally quickly slid the glass of wine back on the shelf in the chicken-house where he had been working. He greeted the minister with a smile. The visit lasted only five minutes, but in that five minutes God fanned the fires of judgment until Wally nearly choked. The preacher laid his hand on his shoulder and prayed a short but pointed prayer and drove away down the hill. It was not very many weeks before Wally and Beverly Walrath each had a personal experience with Jesus Christ. Their sins were forgiven and they tasted the joy of real salvation.

For months following their conversion the Walraths had an old holiness preacher by the name of Reverend Maxwell come to their home on Friday nights and preach to any who might gather in their living room. During those months, a young hippie couple rented the Walrath's little two-room cabin which stood directly up the hill from their house. They were Steven and Sandy Palm. The Walraths took an immediate interest in them spiritually, and soon they were saved.

During the summer of 1968, the Walraths and Palms attended a holiness camp meeting in Orangevale, California. Steven was making great progress spiritually, but Sandy was finding it difficult to seriously agree with the Bible. By the time they got back to Santa Cruz, she was intent on returning to the world. The Walrath's hearts were broken when the young couple moved out of the cabin and separated from each other.

Those fall and winter months were a battle, but the Walraths were determined to build a holiness work. They tried again and again to find a preacher who would come and organize a church.

It was John Miller who finally answered the call. He and his young wife Juanita moved into the two-room cabin. Sunday services were held in the Walrath's living room, Sunday school was taught in the bedrooms, and the Bible Missionary Church was officially organized in Santa Cruz, California.

Every single weekday during John Miller's two-year ministry there, they attended a prayer meeting held in the home of an old Free Methodist preacher named Dozier. Brother and Sister Dozier had been forced into retirement by age and poor health. The old minister could not pastor or preach, but he could pray. And he set himself to pray for a Holy Ghost revival in the Santa Cruz area. For a number of years he had been praying four to eight hours every day.

John Miller said that during those two years, in all those morning prayer meetings, he could only remember twice when they did not come out of the Dozier's home shouting and rejoicing and wiping tears of great victory. Revival was arriving in Santa Cruz.

§§§

Sandy Palm had been traveling alone. She was in Seattle.

48

God had been on her trail ever since she left California and now He had finally gained a new entrance into her heart. When she reached the Walraths on the phone, it was a time of rejoicing.

By the time Sandy arrived back in Santa Cruz, the Walraths had a line on Steven's location. They were sure he was somewhere in the Santa Cruz area. With a little detective work, Beverly and Sandy located him up in the coastal mountains in a shack in the woods. He had been up there for months, living off government commodities and washing in a stream. They persuaded him to come down to the house for supper that evening.

Steven had been washing in a stream, but he had not combed his hair in months. Using cooking lard, he greased it down to what he considered almost presentable and drove his old car down to the Walrath house. As they ate and talked, he felt a yearning in his heart to get right with God. That night he drove his rattletrap down the driveway with the determination to find a place to pray. Far over in Yosemite National Park, high in the Sierra Nevada Mountains, after a day and a half in prayer, Steven's sins were forgiven.

When they heard the old car coming up the driveway two days later, Beverly and Sandy ran out the back door. Steven climbed out with a shine on his face that was clearly from another world. "Guess who's got the victory!" he shouted as his wife ran into his arms.

It wasn't long before some of Steven and Sandy's old hippie friends began to answer invitations to the cottage services on Sundays. One by one many were spiritually awakened under the preaching of young Reverend Miller, and by the genuine love and concern of the growing church.

The Walrath home eventually became the home of many of their converts, with their second bedroom becoming a sort of girls' dorm, and the little basement room the boys' quarters. Wally was working as a marketing executive for a highly technological firm that manufactured space-age machinery. He made good money and it took all he made to keep the little farm operating and everyone fed. At times it seemed the little house would burst at the seams as the lively group worshipped together. Wally and Beverly often stood in amazement as the zealous new Christians filled up their home, taking more and more of their time and energy. They both confessed that they were simply the blest observers of a work which was obviously the sovereign doings of God Himself.

§§§

Ray took a long hit and handed the joint to me.

I was busy looking across the Bay and did not notice.

"Here," he grunted, nudging my arm.

"Oh," I said taking it in my fingers.

"Hey, Brad," he raised his voice, "take a hit, the thing's going out."

"Oh," I said, "yeah."

Chapter Five

OLD WAR STORIES

I graduated from basic training with four things: an expert marksmanship medal, a Private E-1 stripe, orders to report to Seaman School in Fort Eustis, Virginia, and an even greater determination to beat the system and get an early out. It must have been the fact that I followed Ray alphabetically that got me into Seaman School. He had joined the army for a three-year hitch in order to get that trade and I was the only other man in the whole company who got the same assignment. Ray and I were thrilled when we compared orders that morning before graduation.

In our new barracks at Fort Eustis, Ray and I were assigned to the same bay. That first roll call was quite a change from California. It was January, freezing and foggy. We were almost excited until we learned that Seaman School would not start for almost a month, during which time there would be daily work details around the base. I was sent to the supply room to sort laundry with four other disgruntled privates. We spent the greater part of the day sleeping on large mounds of dirty clothes.

I do not remember where they assigned Ray that day, but I do remember one thing: that was the last day either of us spent on a work detail at Fort Eustis. The very next morning found us both heading for sick bay. It was as simple as filling out a short form before breakfast. They called our names at roll call, gave us our passes for the day, and off we went. No telling what we claimed was wrong with us when we got to the doctor; that was non-essential as long as we got our passes and the day off. We were expected to report to the barracks C-Q as soon as we left the infirmary, but we knew as long as we showed up for evening roll call we would never be missed.

A guy can't go to sick call every day, but there were other ways of getting out of work. At morning roll call the next day, Ray and I stood at the rear of the lines of soldiers. When our names were called we gave the appropriate answers. When roll call was completed, and the men were being sent to work details, Ray and I simply slipped out of the rear, strolled casually across the quad to the large barracks opposite ours, walked up the steps, through the doors, across the hallway, out the other doors, down the steps, and off into the great beyond. There was always so much going on, and men going off here and there to work details, it was never questioned if the two inconspicuous soldiers walking confidently along were at all out of place. And what did we do all day? There was the PX, grocery store, hardware store, picture show, restaurant, recreation center, bowling alley, forests to hike in, and a bus station with pinball machines. What a life! The only appointment we had to keep was the evening roll call just before supper, but then the work was over and the fun began for everybody.

Ray and I were both making plans for an early discharge, and I decided to start at once getting mine. The next week I did not eat at all. I finally started getting shaky and weak and I felt like my eyes were bugging out a little. That was the condition I was striving for. It was time to report to sick call. As I got my pass and started toward the infirmary, Ray slipped through the adjacent barracks and met me on the road.

We spent about forty-five minutes in the waiting room before my name was called. The orderly showed me to a little room. There I sat alone. I knew any moment the doctor would come in. I held my hat in both hands, wringing it like a dish rag. I was shaking from lack of food. My nerves were on edge. Everything was just as I had planned it. Now I sat gearing myself up for the doctor who was about to come through the door.

"Brad?" he said pleasantly.

"Yes," I wrung my hat.

"Step in here and have a seat." There was another door out of the room which I now found led to an office. He sat down behind his desk and opened my medical history. I sat wringing my hat, looking out the window. I was shaking.

"What's the trouble?" He leaned back.

I told him I was afraid. I looked at my hat.

"What are you afraid of?"

"Well. . . everybody keeps talking about me."

"Talking about you?" he said kindly. "Who?"

I was afraid to look him in the face. It was such a ridiculous story. I purposefully wrung my hat as I spoke, "Everybody." I was looking out the window. "All the guys in the barracks."

"What do you mean?" he asked. "What do they say?"

"I don't know. . . they whisper." I was starting to get into the act now. "They look and whisper and laugh. . . they laugh at me." I was so nervous that my face actually began to twitch and my voice whimpered. I looked down and sort of started to cry. I was really psyched up. "I can't stand it anymore," I blurted. "I can't stand being in there with all those guys. . . I don't know what to do."

I leaned back and tried to get my breath. He was reading through my records. I knew what was in them: drugs, hospitals, doctors. It was my only hope. He was really studying now, turning pages.

"I see you have a history of drug abuse," he said softly, still looking at my stuff. "Have you been taking anything lately?"

"No."

"When was the last time you took L. S. D?" he said.

"I don't know. I haven't had any since I left California."

"How many times have you taken it?"

"I don't know. Thirty, forty maybe." I said.

He shuffled my papers and looked up, "I can't get you in to a psychiatrist 'til Monday. I'll give you a prescription that should help calm you down."

He ushered me out the door, "Do you think you can make it through the weekend?"

"I think so," I said.

That was Thursday. Ray and I went to the Recreation Center and I had a huge meal.

"Why wait until Monday," I reasoned as we lounged in the comfortable Rec Hall. "I know the doctor was convinced. Why else would he have given me these drugs?" I gave Ray my idea for phase two, something which had just come to me.

"Listen," I started, "What do you think of this. . ." At five-thirty the next morning as everybody was getting ready for the day, I took a large bottle of water, the Seconal, and a jar of aspirin into a private toilet stall. The barbiturates went down easily, as they were in gelatin capsules; but I could only manage about seventy-five aspirins before I was gagging. I threw the bottles in the trash and went back to my bunk.

By the time most of the guys were on their way to breakfast

Ray came over to where I was lying on my stomach, "Hey, Brad, come on," he said loudly. "You'd better hurry, or we'll be late for breakfast."

"I'm not going," I sighed.

We exchanged a few planned words loud enough for some of our nearest barrack mates to hear and then Ray left. I lay facing the wall waiting for the next move. Ray went to the C-Q and told them he thought his friend had taken an overdose.

The sergeant followed him upstairs to my bunk. "Get out of bed, Henshaw!" he growled.

I turned over, looking as drugged as I could; actually I wasn't feeling anything yet. "I'm not getting up," I sighed.

He yanked my covers back and grabbed my elbow, "GET DOWN HERE!"

I rolled out and sat down dreamily on my foot locker, looking at the floor. The sergeant stood before me. "You'd better be dressed in five minutes, Henshaw, or you'll be in the brig!" He strode away.

I was lacing my boots when the sergeant reappeared holding the empty pill bottles and also an empty cough syrup bottle, "Did you take these?"

I looked up dizzily, "I didn't take the cough syrup," I slurred on purpose.

"But you did take these aspirin," he demanded. "And how many of these did you take?" I looked up. He was holding out the empty prescription bottle.

"All of them," I whispered.

"Are you sure you didn't take any cough syrup?"

"No. I didn't take that," I tried to appear to be having trouble getting my boots laced up. Ray had gone to breakfast. The barracks were empty.

"You'd better be there for roll call!" the sergeant snarled as he walked away.

By the time the guys were getting back from breakfast I was standing out in the quad alone. It was beginning to sprinkle in the pre-dawn twilight and the atmosphere was low and balmy. I was standing at attention in the rain, the only person out there. More and more guys began looking out the windows at me and pretty soon Ray came out and asked how I was getting along. I told him I was just starting to feel it.

"Why don't you come back in?" He whispered, "I think the ambulance is on its way."

I followed him back up the steps and through the big doors, getting dizzier all the time. The stairwells were full of soldiers as roll call would be inside, out of the rain. I was halfway up through the crowd when the commotion reached me. "He's right up here!"

"Hey!" shouted a guy in a white suit. "You Henshaw?"

"Yeah."

He looked back down the stairs, "Here he is, Chuck, up here!" Chuck made his way up the crowded stairs. "This is him right here." They had the empty bottles.

By the time they got me to the ambulance, we had drawn quite a crowd. The red lights added to the drama as we sped away in the rain. "How long ago did you take these. . . were they full?" I was beginning to relax. I knew I was in good hands.

In the emergency room I was given a pint of milk and some gooey stuff that looked like honey. The doctor and three orderlies were enjoying the whole thing and chuckled as they showed me a sink where they said I would be spending most of the day. I didn't understand, but before long I knew what they meant as I began my vomiting routine. I must have vomited for three or four hours. I got so overdosed from the Seconal I could not see straight. Everything was spinning wildly. I went from the stretcher to the sink and back again a hundred times. Around ten o'clock I must have passed out or at least become delirious. I could still see lights and color and doctors and orderlies, but my vision was doubled and my mind was in chaos. More than once I wondered if I really was going to die.

About three o'clock that afternoon, I was driven to the psychiatric building. I had to lie down on the couch in the waiting room in order to fill out the form. After a long wait they showed me into the office where I sat in front of the doctor's desk. He asked some questions which I tried to answer the best I could in my condition. I had only been there a few minutes when he made a statement that nearly knocked me out of the chair. "You'll never get out of the Army by trying to kill yourself," he said flatly. I was devastated and nearly lost my composure. I tried to appear unmoved and said nothing.

"About the only way that will work is if you really do kill

yourself." He read my pedigree so perfectly that I wondered if he could read my mind. Still I said nothing. I tried to look as stupid as I could. It was like trying to stare down a wildcat. He told me to get back to my barracks.

I did not feel exactly whipped, it just had not gone as easily as I had figured it would. I did have a good foundation laid and I was going to build on it with everything I could pull off. That weekend I rested up and fattened up a bit. It was the end of round two; I was bloody, but not beaten.

Monday I kept my appointment with the psychiatrist which had been made by the MD who had given me the Seconal. This was a different psychiatrist. He read my file and we talked for about forty-five minutes. The session was not at all satisfactory in my opinion, pretty anticlimactic. I told him everybody was talking about me and all that, but I did not feel as if it had the effect on him that it had on the MD. I left the clinic feeling low.

The next morning I was on a Greyhound headed north to Canada, Absent Without Leave. On Wednesday Jill drove out to Buffalo, New York, to meet me. When we crossed the border at Niagara Falls I presented my "Landed Immigrant" papers to the Canadian authorities and we zoomed on through to Toronto. Thursday I found a room for rent in an old house for fourteen dollars a week, and that very evening I looked up my old employer in Yorkville, and was given another job with Mr. Submarine.

Friday was a bright winter day I was walking through the Village enjoying the crunch of the dry snow under my army boots. With my jeans, field jacket and short hair, I guess "deserter" was written all over me. Someone called out of a second-storey window, "Hey, Yank!" I looked up startled. "You! Yankee! Where you from?"

I was trembling as I answered his invitation upstairs. I sat down next to the window in his messy quarters and heard his story about being a deserter from Missouri. I did finally admit I was a deserter, but I did not like him much and got out of there as quickly as I could.

I was so depressed I could hardly stand it. That night after work, I lay in bed with the light on for hours. I tried to write a poem but could not get anywhere with it. Before I turned off the light I took a couple of bites from the sub I was keeping refrigerated outside on the window ledge. It was frozen.

Those days spent in that little room were horribly depressing. Walking back and forth to Yorkville, eating cold submarine sandwiches and snow-chilled chocolate milk every morning and trying to be poetic, brought on an awful sickness that almost drove me insane. When I talked to my mother on the phone, she promised, if I would go back to Ft. Eustis, she would enlist Dr. Freidman in an all-out campaign in getting me out of the Army. Four days later I was back in Virginia walking up the steps to my barracks C-Q.

It was a Friday evening. I was issued an Article Fifteen (that means you are in trouble and will have to work so many hours extra to pay it off). I was standing in front of the First Sergeant's desk expecting to be put under lock and key. He looked at his watch, "Report to me Monday morning after roll call," he said, "in uniform."

That weekend, Ray and I went to Virginia Beach. We were just a week away from the beginning of Seaman School and thought we would have a big time before we had to get down to work. Monday I reported to the First Sergeant's office right after roll call and he hit the ceiling, "WHERE DO YOU THINK YOU'RE GOING?"

"Nowhere," I answered. "Just reporting as you told me."

"Where's your uniform?"

"In my locker," I answered.

"WELL, WHY DON'T YOU HAVE IT ON?" he bellowed.

"I can't put it on."

"What?"

"I don't feel like I can put it on. I just don't feel right about it."

Round five had begun. "SIT DOWN!" he snapped. Twenty minutes later I was in the Captain's office. On his desk lay my open file. Everywhere I went, there was my file. If you ever see a soldier running across a military installation with a folder under his arm, he has just been sent to get someone's file and is moving it to the necessary location. Here it was, miraculously laying on the Captain's desk.

The Captain interrogated me for a few minutes as I stood

57

before his desk with his Lieutenant at my side. I stuck to the same story about how they were all talking about me.

"How many times have you taken this L. S. D.?" he asked.

"I don't know. Quite a bit, I guess."

"Well, how many? Five, ten, fifteen?"

"Oh," I said, "more than that."

"Twenty?" He raised his eyebrows.

"More," I said.

"Thirty," he was astonished. "Forty?"

"Forty or fifty times, I guess. I don't really know."

He looked at the Lieutenant as if he was amazed I could even stand there. The Lieutenant shook his head piously. Finally, the Captain told him to take me up and see that I shaved and got my fatigues on.

As we were walking down the hall together, the Lieutenant shook his head, "I just can't understand why people won't soldier." He said it as sincerely as a saint.

Having learned I was an artist, they gave me the assignment of designing title pages for the Lieutenant's notebook to pay off my Article Fifteen. In the evenings, I would be sitting at the Lieutenant's desk with a bunch of colored pens; some private would come through sweeping or dusting or mopping and I would look up and take a sip of Coke and say, "What have you got? An Article Fifteen?"

And he would say, "Yeah, what are you doing?"

"Designing title pages for the Lieutenant," I would smile.

"Wow. How'd you get a job like that?"

"Article Fifteen," I would say. He would look at his mop and then at my colored pens. About that time I would take another sip of Coke and he would walk out shaking his head.

I finished the title pages early and since Seaman School was starting that Monday, they let me off my Article Fifteen. During that first week of school, my Captain got orders from the psychiatrist to put me in a semi-private room with no more than three roommates. The next week my three roommates received new orders and were gone, so I had the room all to myself.

Seaman School was divided into two parts. Part "A" lasted four weeks and was composed of learning to tie knots, to drive a troop landing craft, and to run a crane for loading cargo. I graduated at the top of my class.

Between schools "A" and "B" there was a week in which Ray and I had to use the adjacent barracks escape route to keep out of work details. Then by the time school "B" started, I was told by the psychiatrist that I was all right and did not need to continue my weekly appointments unless I started having trouble.

School "B" was mostly classroom stuff. I was keeping my grade average up, but I started feeling like the system was getting a grip on me. I was relaxing my war with Uncle Sam. It began to bother me, and I was afraid if I did not do something quickly, I would start losing points. Ray always seemed to be game for anything, and when he heard my new plan for the next round, he really got a kick out of it.

The previous week we had gone to see a guy who was painting a stripe around his barracks bay. It was a nice red stripe, about three feet wide, all around the perimeter of the large floor. It was done perfectly, a beautiful job. He was at it when we went over and I had asked him why. "I figure it will get me in to see the shrink," he said.

It might and it might not, I thought. Not if his superiors hear his motives. To appear crazy, I figured one must keep things very secret. Ray was my only confidant.

When I gave Ray my new battle plan, I'm sure he knew where I got the idea. "We'll get some paint and some acid, and we'll lock ourselves in my room with your radio and paint one psychedelic mural all over everything. It will be beautiful," I chortled. "Then along about four in the morning we'll paint right out into the hall and down the walls. I can see them now as the bell rings and they all start coming out to the bathroom and, WOW! All down the halls are vines and flowers and bees, and there we are, painting like a couple of cases right out of the nut house."

We located the acid, and then at the hardware store we bought about twenty dollars' worth of every bright color they had. The door to my room had no lock so we pushed the big steel bunk up against it, took the acid, turned on the music and started painting. After a couple of hours, it was smelling like a turpentine factory and we were heading out for a breather; but when we started down the stairs, we found we were so high we were afraid we might get lost and never get back. Returning to the room, we opened the windows and kept at it. It was slower going than we thought, and along about ten o'clock we began to wonder if we would ever get it finished in time to start out into the hall at four o'clock in the morning. So far we had one wall completed including the locker and part of the window frames. As we rested and talked, I suddenly realized I was so high I could not stand it. I had taken much more than a single dose of the L. S. D. and my mind was beginning to get out of hand. The air was full of tiny bubbles so thick I could barely see Ray through them. He was sitting on the bed and prisms were reflecting like rainbows all around him. I looked out the window. It had rained that day and puddles as large as lakes lay across the quad.

"We've got to get out of here," I stuttered. I knew the plan had to be aborted. I had to hit the road. I put on my sandals and Ray picked up his radio and we started to leave.

"What about all this paint we haven't used," he asked. I picked up a pint of royal blue and poured it out across the top bunk where it soaked and ran and dripped.

We walked to the bus station, the only place we could go off base without a pass. We told the gate guard we were going over to play the pin-balls. Then we simply walked in the front door of the bus station and out the back. Once on the open road we stuck up our thumbs into some oncoming headlights, the car stopped and we climbed into the back seat. The stereo system was cranked up so loud it sounded like a live band, one had to yell to be heard.

We had been picked up by a couple of drunk mountain boys in a hot rod. Off they sped, roaring and screeching down a curvy road through the woods. We were scared to death. They said they would take us all the way into Williamsburg, but we asked to be let out early, at a crossroads with one highway light and a few dark buildings. They were mad because we wanted out, but we got away without a fight and started into town on foot, which was not too far up the road.

We were going to head to William and Mary University where we had once spent the day sightseeing. We figured we'd find an open classroom where we could spend the night and then catch a bus the next morning. What we didn't count on was that a policeman was sitting in his squad car watching us dabble in a patch of gutter water under a streetlight, stirring the colorful oil slick.

He was sitting in the dark under a large tree as we walked right by him. "Hello, boys," he spoke like he knew he had a couple of sitting ducks.

"Hi." We approached his car with our hearts in our throats.

"You boys from the base?"

"Yes, sir," we answered quickly.

"Do you have passes?"

"No, sir," I was thinking fast. "We're new at the base. We heard about Williamsburg and thought we could walk over in a few minutes. We got lost and it got dark and so we finally spotted the lights and came toward town. We had no idea it was so far from the base."

"Do you have ID's?"

"Yes, sir," we handed them over and he studied them under his flashlight.

"Why don't you boys get in the back seat while I call headquarters," he said.

The car was as plush as a brand new Cadillac. It had a customized dash that looked like an office. He sat back like an executive behind his desk and talked on a push-button phone. After giving our names and serial numbers, there was silence as he waited for the return call.

I said casually, "We were really looking forward to seeing the town. I hear it's full of historical buildings and stuff."

"Well," he said, "it will be a while before the MP's get out here for you. Why don't I just give you a little tour on our way to the station?"

We were just closing our doors and he was preparing to start up when a speeding car came racing down a cross street. "Hold on, boys, we're going for a ride!"

He pulled out into the road and around the corner and put it to the floor. The car he was after was quite a distance ahead by now I punched Ray in the leg and he grinned like the Cheshire cat. The squad car had an engine to match the high class interior. It literally lifted off the ground when the carburetor opened up. It sounded like a jet turbine. He must have been getting a real kick out of it; we were a couple of lost boys and he was giving us the show of our lives. He never even put the headlights on, we just went out through the country like an invisible rocket.

Earlier, the drunks in the jalopy had scared us to death, but now we had nothing to fear but the coming MP's and we would meet that when it came; right now we were having a whale of a good time. The combination of the high-speed chase, the hallucinogens, and the opulent back seat of the police cruiser made for the ultimate carnival ride. When he caught up to the other car, he flicked a switch, and all the lights and siren came on at once. The car pulled over.

He was only out of the cruiser for a minute when he returned and the other car moved off into the darkness. "Friend of mine," he said. "Lives out here a couple of miles."

He took us back to town and began pulling up to old houses and buildings and turning on his spotlight, showing us the historical points of interest and telling us all he knew about them. It was obvious that he was proud of his town and glad to be giving us the grand tour. We wound around and around until we finally pulled up in front of the police station and were ushered into a modest old building and told to have a seat and wait for the MP's.

"They're OK," he told the man at the desk, "just lost. They're not drunk or anything." We were hallucinating all over the place.

The MP's who drove us back to the base were just as unsuspecting as the Williamsburg police. After a few minutes at the base police station, they were told to drive us back to our barracks and drop us off.

"Well, here you go," said the driver when he pulled up in front of our building. "Since you weren't drunk or anything, we'll just leave you off here."

We got out and watched them drive away. I looked at Ray, "Wow, just like that." We walked quietly through the big front doors and up the stairs to the second floor and my room. As we opened the door, the smell of turpentine engulfed us. I was not ready for what I saw. It seemed like centuries since we had left.

"Look at it," Ray said with his mouth standing open. "Man, we'd better get out of here while the gettin's good." We were straight enough now to know it would never do to try to resume our plan.

It would be impossible to describe all the swirls and

patterns and designs that decorated the walls, windows, and lockers. Paisleys, stars, flares, vehicles, beings — then there was the blue bunk bed and smeared floor and open paint cans. It was a cross between cannibal art and dynamite.

The garb I had on was not practical for traveling in the open. I quickly changed into long underwear, jeans and a heavy shirt. Then I put on some rubber-soled civilian shoes, a navy blue knit cap, and made sure I had all my money and ID. Then we shut her up.

Ray got reasonably arranged, and we went straight for a phone booth outside the base bar where we called the Newport News Taxi. He was there in a few minutes and we were on our way to the Newport News bus station where, at sunrise we caught a bus for New Orleans.

Chapter Six

ABSENT WITHOUT LEAVE

The sun was rising on April Fool's Day, 1970, when the bus pulled out of Newport News. Ray and I rode together all that day and well into the night. We had to change buses in Atlanta, Georgia, with about a two-hour layover, and it was while sitting in the terminal that Ray told me he had made the decision to go back to New Jersey and visit his mother. Ray had lived with his father in California since his parents divorced; his mother was ill and he hated to be this close and not see her at least once. I was surprised, but understood his reasoning and did not argue with him. The thing I had to face now was whether to go on alone to the west coast, or go back with Ray. It was monumental. I felt so lonely, but there was something akin to manhood that rose up in me and demanded that I keep with my plan, that to do otherwise would prove me a coward and a kid. It never entered my mind what an awful coward and kid I was being already.

We said good-bye and I watched Ray leave on a northbound bus. Not only was I now enjoying the exhilaration of liberty, but I was also faced with the responsibility of independence. It was not without trembling that I headed south alone that night.

In the wee hours of the morning, we pulled into the station in Birmingham, Alabama. After I got a snack I was confronted by a lady who was handing out religious tracts at the door of the bus. I took one and climbed up to my seat. I watched her out the window as I drank my Coke. I thought, "How embarrassing. How could she do that, right there in the bus station?" I looked at the outside of the tract and stuck it in my shirt pocket. She was hitting everybody who came near. They treated her like she had the plague, but everybody took one, nonetheless.

We were well on the road and my snack was all gone. I took the tract out of my pocket for lack of anything else to do. There was a picture at the top of the front fold. I was not much for reading, but I finally browsed through the first paragraph. It was a story about a boy who was in trouble, and by the second paragraph I was drawn right into the story. I followed his life of pain and sorrow. It was a pathetic story, but the end was joyful, with him finding Jesus and salvation and a wonderful new life. I was so alone and the Alabama night was so dark that I just let go right there in the front seat — nobody saw as I finished the last paragraph and tears ran down my cheeks. I looked out the big front windows with blurry eyes. I was a long way from home, not only geographically, but morally and mentally. I had broken down every fence of my childhood training. I had faced captains and doctors. I had fought and rebelled, hated and deceived. I was no longer a college kid from a middle-class home; I was absent without leave, running from crimes committed against God and country. The tears continued as I read the tract again.

New Orleans was the end of the line as far as the bus went for me, since I was down to twenty dollars. Mike and Libby, some old friends from Bakersfield, were stationed in New Orleans in the Navy and were glad to hear from me and came immediately to the bus station. I spent the night in their little apartment and tried to explain what I was doing, and why. They were pretty good kids, it was impossible for them to understand. The next morning they drove me out by the airport where I could get a ride west.

I made it to Houston that night. About ten o'clock a guy in a nice El Camino picked me up on a freeway on-ramp. His music was playing and I was relaxing when he reached over and pushed a button on the radio. All of a sudden it sounded like I was sitting in a police car. He looked like any guy out for a night on the town. I listened a minute more. I knew it was a cop radio.

"Are you a policeman?" I asked right out.

"Yes." And after a long moment, "I'm a plain-clothes policeman." That was all he said. He knew what he was doing to me mentally. I was certain I was headed for the station when he asked me where I wanted to go. I said I really did not know and acted like I was thinking about getting a motel. He made some suggestions and finally let me out in downtown Houston.

I located a Salvation Army place, and paid sixty cents at the door. A man with a flashlight showed me to the third floor, and a huge bay of a room full of cots and sleeping men. There must have been fifty beds at least. It was dark. Many men were already asleep. The place stunk so bad, I thought I would not be able to endure it; it was like holding an old man's dusty, dirty, sweaty sock over your nose.

I stripped to my long military underwear, put my clothes under the cot and my valuables under my pillow and managed about five hours sleep. At six we were rousted out and I was allowed to take a shower.

I walked out that morning without any idea where I was in Houston or how to get on the road west. I could see a freeway overpass and walked over a couple of streets to where I could read one of the signs; it was Interstate 10, just the one I wanted. How to get on it was another question I finally found a vehicle on-ramp, but at six-thirty a.m. there wasn't any traffic for a ride. I realized I was breaking the law as I walked out on the freeway on foot, but I felt I had no recourse. The highway was like a ghost town. The very first car that came by stopped and gave me a good ride to the western edge of Houston.

I had not waited very long before a couple of cowboys in a hot rod stopped on their way to Austin. Then north of Austin I got a ride with a college girl for a ways and then an older couple on into Sonora. There I got a hamburger and walked out to the western end of town and set up for a ride. By that I mean I found a place where cars could get a good look at me in enough time to stop, with available space to pull over. There I spent a long two hours and was getting pretty depressed when it began to rain. I started back into town on foot, still holding my thumb out to the traffic. A guy in a Volkswagen stopped right where I was standing at the curb. His window was down on my side and I looked in.

"How far you going?" I said with my hand on the door handle.

"Los Angeles," he smiled.

"Wow!" I pulled the door open, "If you don't mind, you've got a rider all the way."

That morning in the Salvation Army I had rolled up my long johns and knotted them, and had been carrying it like a ball all day. It was now lying on my lap. WOW! All the way to L.A.! I pitched it out the window into the West Texas desert.

That night I slept on the floor in an air conditioned motel room in El Paso. The next night we were just outside San Diego where he got a room in a Howard Johnson's. I was trying to sleep on some chair cushions on the floor, but got so cold without any blankets that I decided to try the bathroom which had a heat light in the ceiling. It was a small room, and the only place I could find to stretch out was in the tub, which wasn't too bad with the cushions. The problem was having to get up and re-set the heat-light timer every hour or so.

I knew my old college chum Joe had moved back into our same apartment building in Seal Beach. It was about eleven that next morning when my ride dropped me off right at his door. I spent a week there and then headed to Bakersfield.

Mom and Dad were shocked when I showed up out of the blue, they thought I was in Virginia. I know I worried them greatly. I sometimes wonder how they stood it, and I'll always appreciate their love and patience.

One of the first things Mom wanted me to do was go to Doctor Freidman. I was all for that as I was hoping he would help me get out of the Army. He heard my long story and then wrote a letter to the Army for me.

I took the letter and went up to the Mojave Desert and turned myself in at Edwards Air Force Base. After three days in the Air Force jail, I was taken by MP's to Fort MacArthur in Long Beach to be transferred to Fort Eustis, Virginia, for punishment.

It was about seven in the evening when we got to the coast and Ft. MacArthur. Some other prisoners and I were ushered into a small building which was a military police transfer station. There we sat behind bars as one-by-one we were called out to the desk, given instructions and turned over to guards. When my turn came, the sergeant read my papers and said that since I had turned myself in, I could have special privileges. I could stay in a regular barracks and even go into town if I wanted. All I had to do was show up at seven o'clock in the morning to pick up my airplane ticket to Ft. Eustis.

I got a local bus into Long Beach and called Joe from the Greyhound station. In thirty minutes he was there to pick me up. I do not know what made me jump again. I just could not face going back to Ft. Eustis and all the trouble that awaited me there. I also knew that if I did not continue to do irrational things, they would never be convinced of my insanity. At this point, I felt I had earned a pretty good (or bad) record, and I hated to compromise it.

After a week at Joe's, I called home and got a promise from

Doctor Freidman that if I came to Bakersfield he would put me in the hospital.

I spent twelve days in the Kern General Psych Ward before the Army came and got me. They took me and two guys they had picked up from the county jail to the airport where we were handcuffed and flown to Monterey in a twin-engine private plane. As we circled Monterey Airport, I could see Fort Ord just to the north. The little city of Monterey sat like a lookout on its beautiful rocky point guarding the southern rim of the bay. Far to the north, the mountains behind Santa Cruz lay in repose.

The Fort Ord MP's picked us up at the Monterey Airport and drove us to the Special Processing Detachment (SPD) to await court martial, sentencing, hospitalization, discharge, or whatever. Business was over for the day when we got there and so we were held in a high-security barracks for the night. About ten o'clock one of the guys sneaked out the window and over the fence. I expected to be put in the hospital the next morning so I slept with relative peace of mind.

Special Processing Detachment was a sort of vacation land for Army dropouts. There were twelve barracks (one of which was the mess hall) all enclosed by a ten-foot high chain-link fence with barbed wire around the top. There was a large gate with a guard shack at each end of the two-hundred-yard compound. Army bases are usually the hottest dope-peddling centers in the country, and SPD was the dope center for the base itself. During my first twenty-four hours in SPD, I bought three hits of LSD.

In the next couple of days I could see I was not on my way to the hospital, so I traded the acid for a pair of civilian jeans which were too large and a red-and-white tee shirt that was too small. The fourth morning I wore these under my fatigues and put in for sick call. I showed my pass to the guy in the guard shack, and walked off across the base. In a men's public rest room I got rid of my fatigues — then thumbed a ride to the little town of Seaside. From there it wasn't long before I was over the mountain in Monterey and headed for the Big Sur coastline.

Late that afternoon, a truck full of hippies picked me up. I jumped in the back under a little homemade shed with three guys and a couple of dogs. They had been to town for groceries and were heading back to their "river commune" up in the Big Sur

Mountains. It did not take long for me to explain my predicament, and it did not take long to accept their invitation to come and live with them in the mountains.

There was plenty of sunlight left as we hiked up one of the great canyons that cut into the tremendous cliffs of Big Sur and carried spring water down from the summits. We walked a mile or two up the stony cascade around giant boulders and across fallen redwoods until we came to their "river commune"; it was simply three campsites spotted up the canyon. In the camp highest up the stream lived a married couple and in the next camp down lived a single guy who was sort of a loner and philosopher. The next camp down was full of single guys, and with me it held six.

That night a black man, named Leo, cooked supper over an open fire. Then we all settled down for a set of jug-band music with Leo on the recorder (flute-like instrument) and the rest of us on anything handy for making music and noise. The next morning Leo cooked hot cakes and afterward Mark and I hiked up to a large pool where we washed and splashed and had a great time. It all seemed like a regular Utopia and maybe would have been had I not had a blackness of deep depression in my heart. I just could not feel at home with these people. I knew that no matter how long I might live with them, I could never get close enough to trust them.

That afternoon Leo took me over the creek and up the other side, where he showed me another campsite where no one was residing. It was a nice perch overlooking most of that part of the canyon which was all under the shade of a great sequoia forest. The redwoods were so high that there was a feeling of expanse and depth of field even under their canopy. The unique thing about the deserted campsite was that it had running water. Whoever had originally set it up, had carried a long plastic hose up the canyon. From the camp it ran along the side of a tributary gorge at enough of an angle to meet the feeder brook above the camp; water ran through it in a continuous stream.

On up the mountain Leo led me to yet another camp. This one was out from under the redwoods and sat in the sunshine at the upper end of a small meadow-like clearing. There were thick manzanitas growing along the upper sides of the meadow, and the redwood forest stood along the lower sides. It had been tilled at one time and gave the impression of a primitive little farm. There was a small building of two rooms framed with natural lumber out of the woods. The siding was old, rough plywood and anything else that might keep out most of the elements. There were no doors, just openings in the walls. A married couple had lived there the season before, but had not been seen for several months. The garden was overgrown with the natural flora of the mountains, but clear regular furrows ran the length of the meadow down to the shadow of the forest.

During my third day in Big Sur, we were sitting around the fire after a slow breakfast when a stranger walked into camp from the upper direction of the canyon. He was clean-cut and had on sturdy clothes and expensive hiking boots.

"Hi!" Mark smiled broadly as was his manner. "Have a cup of coffee."

"Hello," said the stranger. He wore no smile. "I'm not here for the company. I've been sent up here by the owner of this property to ask you people to leave." He called the owner's name and made it clear that we were trespassing on private property and that he would follow us down the canyon to make sure we got out.

"It'll take us a little while to get our stuff ready," said Leo; but there was no argument in the issue. The stranger disappeared into the forest and we slowly began to get our gear together. I did not know how my friends would react, but after a few minutes I realized they were going to leave as ordered. There was some talk about coming back in a week or two, but the justice of the thing was clear to all. We were trespassers. It was not something new. We were trespassers wherever we went; on highways, in stores, at gas stations, and now even in the deep of the redwood forest we were the enemies of civilization. "NO HIPPIES ALLOWED" read more than one sign over more than one door along the California coast.

The couple from the highest camp soon came through, having received their eviction before we had; the philosopher was with them. I was the newest of the crowd and had very little gear of my own. I had traded Mark my field jacket for a light brown military dress coat of some sort and it was about all I owned at the time.

They were talking about the inevitability of the situation and figured after the heat was off, it would be safe to return. The huge canyon was private property all right, but no owner lived within miles of it, that was for sure, as there were no roads nor dwellings in the area at all. The general consensus was that if kept quiet in the future, the settlement might yet survive.

Another matter of conversation as we started down the rocky creek was the great fandango that was being planned for that very evening at some ranch on the coast; they had been talking about it ever since I had arrived. It had been heralded far and wide that a tremendous bash was in store for all the freaks and friends of the Big Sur Mountains. So at least we knew where we were headed that day.

§§§

The ranch sat peacefully out above the Pacific Ocean on a long grassy arm of land that seemed to reach miles into the sea, its lower edges were bordered by the omnipresent redwoods. All the ranch amounted to was a modest farmhouse, a good sized garden and a dirt road. There were already scores of cars and pickups parked out in the yellow grass along the dirt road, and the hot afternoon sun was reclining as we made our way toward the party. Music filled the countryside and more than two hundred people of all ages and types covered the grounds. There were rich and poor, children and dogs, Spanish, Caucasian and Negro; they were colorful, gay, creative people. Many were friends and many were strangers; some sat alone and some laughed in large groups; some wandered through the crowd and some played with Frisbees and beach balls. There was a band on the front porch composed of a xylophone, two or three guitars, conga drums and bongos; people were playing woodblocks and sticks and many were simply clapping with the thick rhythms. The music was definitely Mexican and was lusty and free. There was a great crowd that sat like an audience across the wide front yard facing the band, and up at the far end of the yard a pit had been dug over which a tremendous pig was roasting above hot coals.

I was a stranger, but found room among those on the lawn where I sat and tried to take it all in. I had never seen such a happening in all my life. It was the epitome of the word "festive." It was gala.

71

There were all sorts of people mingled together and it was easy to tell they were from various walks of life, from farmers to students, housewives to hippies. But there was one thing they all had in common, they were all freaky. I was in the midst of a great gathering of the hip. Marijuana was passing through the crowd, and wine and beer were in abundance.

From around the side of the house came a man I figured to be the host. He was somewhere in his fifties, grey-headed, tall and distinguished, and carried a tray of food from which he served the people sitting on the lawn. He was smiling and talking and having a grand old time. He was also bare naked and as brown as a bean. He made his way to the pit where he took over the final preparations of the pig that must have been roasting since dawn. It wasn't long before everyone present had a hearty hunk of pork in one hand and homemade bread in the other.

As the evening waxed on, I got acquainted with some guys who were splitting up a bit of acid. On into the wee hours of the night, I tripped from the food to the music and then back to the lawn to lay and gaze up through the heavens. The music went on and on without a break, hour on end. When one musician would tire, he would lay his instrument down and whoever might feel like it, would pick it up and join in the melee.

The crowd had thinned some by midnight, but clear up through two, three and four o'clock the rhythm of the fandango rocked on. By four only a few stragglers wandered about or stood staring into the live coals in the pit. The small band was still jamming intensely on the porch where dust and cigarette smoke filled the air, reminding me of a late-night cock fight. Out on the large lawn there were a few who slept under the dark summer sky.

Just before dawn, I walked back out to where the cars were parked in the field. There were still a dozen or more sitting here and there, and the silence of the sleepers could be felt as the sky began to grey. The guys I had ridden with were asleep in a large van; I climbed in the front seat to try to get some sleep before the day got under way. But all I could do was sit leaning on the steering wheel staring out across the ranch. I was as weary as a dying man. My neck ached and my eyes were pasted slam open. My mouth was dry and tight and my feet were cold. Sleep was all I desired, total escape from the day that was rising on me. My mind throbbed as I stared blankly into the fog that was rolling in from the dawning sea. The mountain was silent.

§§§

Tired as a dog, I hitchhiked down the coast that morning. Every hour seemed like an age. I got across the coastal range at San Louis Obispo, and by the time the sun was scorching the desert, I was sitting in the sand where highways 41 and 46 meet in the middle of nowhere. There wasn't a square inch of shade for miles. I got up as close to the highway sign as I could, but the sun was directly overhead. I was roasting.

As I sat waiting for a ride, I felt like I was becoming another person. I guess it was the odd-fitting clothes that were so far from what I would have chosen by my own personal taste that made the contrast even greater. This whole life situation I was locked into was as strange as a nightmare. Any comfort and security I had enjoyed in the past were gone. Home was only a remote tie with what I used to be. I was so different now that even the thought of home brought feelings of estrangement. I was a freak, an AWOL hippie, and a lonely, solitary person sitting in the burning California sunshine. I was not proud of myself, but even shame was not enough to get me to quit my war with the establishment now.

When a person experiments with insanity and challenges every ethic established by God and man, he is in danger of losing the very moorings of reality. I had been putting on a pretty good show ever since I had been drafted, but now it was losing the qualities of a show. Just where did my quest for an early discharge end and my own personal sane mind begin?

It was five o'clock that evening when I knocked on the front door of my parents' apartment. It was the first time I had ever knocked on that door. I had always just walked in. But now I was no longer sure if I would be welcome there.

I had not slept in two days and I had not eaten since the fandango twenty-four hours before. My nervous system had just enough LSD sparking around in it to make me a borderline mental case, and when I sat down in the den with my mom and dad, I went to pieces. I bawled and shook and buried my head in my hands and promised to kill myself if I did not get out of the Army. It was a put-on, of course. Or was it? I bellowed like a coward and an idiot. I'll never know how close I came to actually losing my mind completely in my war with Uncle Sam.

In three days I was sitting in the waiting room of the Fort Ord Mental Health Facility. My parents were inside talking to the doctor. Finally my name was called and I joined them. After a few minutes of conversation, the doctor put it on the line, "If you'll stay put in SPD, I promise I'll have you out of the Army inside of two weeks."

I said nothing.

"I'm a short-timer," he said. "In two months I'll be going home. I don't like the Army either, but at least now I'm ready to get out." It sounded funny coming from a Lieutenant, but I'd found out long before that you can't make sense out of what a psychiatrist says.

After a few weeks of 'staying put' in SPD, my papers for discharge arrived. But I could not be found on the work detail. It wasn't until after supper that my barracks sergeant called me into his office and chewed me out for not being there that morning.

"If you wanted out of the army so bad, you should have been here!" he screamed. All the guys were looking on. I was standing at the sergeant's door, the place was electric. "I could send these papers back, you know!"

He stared hatefully at me for a minute and then handed me the papers and turned around. I ran and whooped down the large aisle in the center of the barracks.

The next day I got an early start going through the many lines in the red-tape process of getting discharged. It was a long day, and I was coming down to the last station which was finance. I already had my official discharge in hand, and thought finance would be a waste of time in my case. I skipped the long line at the station just before finance and moved directly to the finance window.

"Where's your paper from the last station?" asked the lady at the finance wicket."

I skipped it," I said.

"You know you've got to go through there before you can get your money?" she asked.

"Yes," I answered, "but I don't expect I'll be getting any money. I didn't want to wait through that line if I didn't have to. You couldn't tell me if I have anything coming, could you?"

She ran her finger down the list and when she got to my name she read, "Two hundred-forty dollars and seventy-two cents."

"I'll be right back," I said, turning from the window and running to the previous line.

Two hours later I was climbing on the Fort Ord Greyhound and heading for home.

§§§

(*At the end of the book you will find my letter of restitution to the Army, and the response.)

Chapter Seven

THE VIOLENT TAKE IT BY FORCE

The battle was raging. I was so vitally connected to three worlds that I was being torn apart mentally. My awareness of God was becoming an almost pathological concentration. I was locked so straightly into drugs that it was with religious fanaticism that I kept my chemical devotions. At times I recognized the immediate presence of spirit beings crowding in on me. In the midst of all this confusion, the earth became my basic truth. My communion with the spirit world would leave me charred and exhausted. With my whole heart I was seeking fellowship with the Creator — and at the same time, I was being whipped and burned by the seductive spirits of the damned.

Shortly after my discharge, I returned to Seal Beach where I was daily on the seashore, staring out across the Pacific, groaning for location, weeping for answers to the riddle of life. I spent hours combing the beach for ancient shells and pretty coral, dreaming of an honest relationship with the One Who created them and washed them up on my coast like treasures. I remember climbing up over the huge granite stones of the jetties with the warm sun embracing me and the crisp sea breeze refreshing my senses. Down under the jetty in the damp sand, I studied the starfish and crabs existing in their low-tide societies. Earth! What an appreciation I had for it. And what an awful hunger to be acquainted with the God of the universe.

I am a lucky stone
a pretty shell
He noticed me
and took me to His home
I sit together
there about His room
with all His other treasures
I blow a song to the breeze
and walk along the sand
I add another tear
to the salty sea

and He remembers every one

§§§

Just across from the bottom of our steps, under the next apartment, a mother cat had been weaning a litter of strays. Sometimes the kittens would make it up the steps and cry at our door, but they were always driven away. Strays! Soon they had all found their ways into different homes and were gone, all except one. He was the stray of strays, the last loser; even his mother had gone on to greener pastures leaving him alone to fare for himself. He was skinny and bony and had always stood out from the others as the most wild and fearful. I thought he would finally find a home, but there he was day after day running under the house whenever anyone came near and then peeking out wild-eyed. We called him "Skitzo."

I was discharged on grounds of a "Latent, Residual Schizophrenia," and I had a good idea how the little creature felt. I named him and began to identify with his existence. I wanted to help him, but he was so wild no one could get close enough to even reason with him. He would cry at the door in hunger, and when we opened, he would fly down the steps in fear.

One day (it was the day my $240.72 ran out.) I decided I would win that cat. I took my last dollar to the corner store and bought a coke and a can of cat food. Then I sat on the bottom step and waited.

He smelled the food I had plopped outside his hole and came nervously out for a taste. It was the real thing, meat. He looked over at me and darted back under the house.

I plopped down another chunk and returned to the step. This time it didn't take him nearly so long to appear. In a gulp he had the meat and was gone. I put another chunk in the same place, then another and another right across the way to where I was sitting. He took the first, then the next, then the next, and then he looked at me. I was still as a mountain. He took a couple more. He was now fifteen feet out of his hole, his little tail was standing straight up in fear.

I had a dish placed between my feet. It was tough on the little fellow, but the food was too much to resist. He ate the bits across the walk and then faced me, trembling. He sneaked slowly up to the dish and started in like a lion, gulping down chunks as big as he could, until he was as round as a tennis ball. I carefully picked him up and loved him and soothed him until he quit shaking. Someday, I thought, I'm going to climb up in God's great big lap and rest. Forever.

Skitzo was my dear friend as long as I lived in Seal Beach. He remained a stray, as did I. He lived under the house next door and ran from everyone and everything that moved. But he always came to me, and we would sit and discuss the complexities of life.

§§§

One day I tore a loaf of bread into pieces and scattered it on the sand. Before long the gulls noticed; first one, then two more, then ten. Soon there were over a hundred circling, spinning, and diving. I sat just close enough to prevent their landing and gorging. They had to reach and grab with their dipping beaks as they flew. Like a great crisscrossing cloud, they wheeled back and forth and up and down; the sound of a hundred feathered wings catching the wind, fanning, hissing; their pealing laughter like rusty gate hinges resounding across the sky.

Finally the bread was gone, and the gulls had taken flight. As I headed back up the beach I saw a wiry little man with long, bushy hair coming down to the water with a child on his shoulders. That morning he was a stranger to me, but almost everybody in Seal Beach knew him as "Papa John". As I fell into the happenings that summer, I came to know him quite well. He was only thirty-five years old, but his life had been hard, he looked at least fifty. His old teeth were stained and crooked, and his scraggly beard was grey. I never saw him in anything more than his cut-off jeans. The story was that he had gotten sick of the rat race and dropped out completely, leaving a good job and a family somewhere back East. He was now a leader of the reckless young people in Seal Beach, brown as an Indian and just about as wild. Anything hip and crazy had Papa John at the center of it.

One night we had a fire going in the sand where a crowd of local freaks had gathered for homemade music. There was a guitar and a bass fiddle; I had my harmonica, and there were woodblocks and sticks and hands to clap. It was almost as festive as the fandango on the Big Sur ranch. People began to swarm in like June-bugs around a warm window and it wasn't long before the Seal Beach Police were on the scene.

Papa John was clomping a pair of woodblocks as he walked up to the leading officer. Face to face stood the heads of the opposing factions. The officer was telling us we would have to disperse and Papa John, still keeping the rhythm on his woodblocks, was arguing the point of our freedom to assemble peaceably for any purpose. The crowd was large and clearly stood against the authorities. I guess the cop got a little nervous and not knowing what else to do, he arrested Papa John. There were screams of protest and clenched fists as they drove him off to the police station. The next day Papa John was back on the beach reporting that they had charged him with assault on an officer of the peace. The whole town was incensed. "Assault!" we roared. And so it was: Assault with woodblocks in the first degree.

Papa John defended himself in a crowded courtroom. He was found guilty and had to pay a stiff fine. That made him even more of a hero on the beach and a stronger leader for the anti-establishment.

When I first came under Papa John's spell, he was living with a young couple from Alberta, Canada, who had homesteaded a piece of property in the Southern Canadian Rockies. Now they were in the States and the guy was working in a welding and mechanic shop getting the experience he needed for life in the wilderness. Although they were not married, they had a little girl and were unashamedly expecting a visit from the woman's husband who had stayed in Canada on the property, complying with homesteading laws. When the husband finally appeared, I was surprised to see the apparent harmony they all shared — husband, wife, boyfriend, and boyfriend's daughter.

As the little house would not hold them all, Papa John had to go. Fortunately, he had an old friend who was a forest ranger in the summer and kept an empty apartment in Seal Beach for his winters. It was a bright, sunny bachelor's quarters over a garage, with windows all around and a big tree that stood over it in the yard, giving the impression of a tree house.

It was up in that tree-house that Papa John taught me to cast the "I Ching" (a Chinese religious technique). I had tried some of the Eastern religions already, but this was the first time for the I Ching. I had my own personal approach to any religious idea, which was to direct my prayer and thought to the Creator of the universe, the God of the Bible, the Father of Jesus Christ. No matter if it was Transcendental Meditation, LSD, Paramahansa Yogananda, or what, I knew there was only one true and living God, the Father of Jesus Christ, and it was toward Him that I steered my spiritual energies.

I found 'just the right place' on the floor of the tree house, sat down, crossed my legs and closed my eyes, trying to relax and also concentrate on the Creator. I cast the three coins out onto the floor. By a certain heads-tails formula, arrived at by casting the three coins three times, Papa John found in the book of I Ching the passage I was to read and apply to myself. It was all done very ceremoniously.

He gave me the book opened to the proper passage. I read aloud something which intimated very pointedly that I would someday become a spiritual leader. MY! Papa John was greatly impressed and made a big deal out of it, boosting my ego. But it never really inspired me as being true.

§§§

While Joe and I were sunning on the beach one afternoon, a couple of clean-cut boys came working their way through the bathers with tracts. They knelt down where we were and asked if they could talk to us about Jesus. We consented, and they showed us a tract with a picture of a circle representing man's life. Outside the circle was Jesus and inside the circle were black dots all in confusion. In the center of the circle was a throne, and Self was on the throne. One of the boys said that this was what life without Jesus was like. Then he showed us another circle with the dots arranged in an orderly fashion and Jesus on the throne. He said that was the Christian life, and testified how happy he was serving the Lord. He said we were the only ones on the beach who had listened to him at all. Then he prayed with us as we bowed our heads right there on the sand. But Christianity was a dead issue to me. My belief that Jesus was the Son of God was strictly historical. I'd seen tracts and heard the Gospel. What I wanted was to get face to face with God. These guys were sincere, I knew that — all Christians were sincere. I wanted more than sincerity, more than history. I wanted a genuine introduction to the Person, the Absolute Being, the Living God.

§§§

It had been a late night for a lot of people. Our apartment was cluttered with sleeping souls. I was lying on the floor still wide awake. I had been wide awake when the last dog died a couple of hours ago, and now the day was just beginning to turn the windows grey. I tiptoed quietly out the door, down the steps and to the street. A thin fog covered the beach. The ocean was like glass. I went right to the water and let the little waves wash up around my ankles and pull sand out from under my heels. "Oh, if I could just sink down in the sand and disappear."

It was barely day as I ambled down the water's edge toward the jetty. My heart was aching as if it had been shelled by heavy artillery, gaping open, black and smoky, ragged, torn. There was a lump in my throat as I looked out upon the surf, grey in the early morning mist. As if speaking to the ocean itself, I tried to communicate my grief to God.

"What am I doing?" I said out loud. "Where am I supposed to be going with my life?" The slick little waves lapped and smacked as I walked toward the jetty.

"What's life all about anyway?" I raised my voice, "What am I doing here?" I was standing looking out to the horizon, hands thrust down into my pockets. "God!" I snapped, "I know You're out there! I know You hear me!"

I walked on. Something welled up in my breast that was almost like anger. It wasn't anger though, it was violence. Violence! "WHAT'S THIS LIFE ALL ABOUT!" I shouted. "What am I doing here? Why me? This ocean? This sand? This sky?"

When I got to the jetty, the sun had not yet risen, but here and there the gulls had begun to screech. I laid down on my back in the sand and watched the blue sky begin to show through the drifting clumps of fog. The crisp morning air was salty and my eyes began to smart. Stubbornly I held them open against the wind until water sprang over my vision. The tears were the natural function of my eyes, but when they trickled down the sides of my face they became another kind of tear. A deep emotional well sounded in my heart as I squeezed my eyes shut. Something triggered inside me. I began to sob, great uncontrollable sobs from my very soul. I was all alone out there on the sand and I just let 'er go. Tears coursed down the sides of my head as I cried out like a lost child. Finally the deep-chested sobs abated and I took a wide clearing breath, stuttering as I exhaled, "Oh, God," I prayed with fists clutching the sand. "Please help me."

last night I saw a sick old man
putting on his same old boots
before he tied the first bow
he stopped to weep no place to go

§§§

I don't know what I'm seeing
but I'm looking for God in it

Chapter Eight

THE GOLDEN EDSEL

Soon after my money from the Army ran out, I located a job at the Edgewater Inn as a bellboy. It was a great job and I loved it. There was always money from tips and a paycheck at the end of the week, and there was something different to do every day. I showed people to their rooms, drove the motel station-wagon, set up rooms for conventions, and hung letters on the big sign out on Pacific Coast Highway.

I moved out of Seal Beach and into my own apartment just off the Long Beach shores. It was a huge apartment compared to the one Joe and I had been sharing, Spanish in decor, with a beautiful enclosed garden and patio just outside my door. I had all my own art on the walls, and treasures sitting around everywhere. But the financial pressures were heavy and I had no ability to manage finances. One week I found myself so broke that I gave a pint of blood for money to buy peanut butter and bread.

The week before Halloween I was up on the towering sign taking down the letters of welcome which had been for some convention. I had been told to leave the sign blank as there was nothing new to promote, but while up there, more for a joke than anything, I hung the letters, "WELCOME GREAT PUMPKIN."

The following two days were my days off. About ten o'clock the next morning I was out for a walk in the October sunshine when a car horn sounded and I heard someone yelling my name. I turned to see an old Edsel with arms waving wildly out the windows. They made a "U" turn on a side street and pulled up to where I was standing. I was wondering who these people were when I spotted Jim, a guy with whom I had made friends in the Army in SPD just a few months earlier. I hadn't seen Jim since my discharge and was thinking what a coincidence it was to see him in Long Beach, but he said they had come through town looking specifically for me.

"I told you he was far out," he grinned to his friend, apparently making a point. "Didn't I tell you he was so high we would probably be drawn together by cosmic energy?"

We went down to the beach for a while, and I learned they

83

were on a trip through Southern California selling THC (a powerful psychedelic drug composed of the chemical equivalence of marijuana). They had driven down from the northern part of the state the day before and were on a money-making tour. They invited me to go along.

"I'd love to," I said, "but I have to be at work the day after tomorrow."

"Tomorrow we plan to be with some people in Fullerton," Jim said. "That's not too far from here, is it?"

"An hour or two," I guessed.

"We'll get you back to work on time," Jim urged. "Come on, Brad, the quicker we get out of here, the more time we'll have for San Diego this afternoon."

I swallowed one of the tablets of THC they were peddling and off we headed. By the time we got to Corona Del Mar I was so high I couldn't see straight. They were getting tired of trying to drive so we pulled over and parked next to a field across which we made for the beach. We had gotten about half way when a horn honked and we looked around to see a California State Police car sitting behind the "Golden Edsel." My heart stopped. There I was with a bunch of dope dealers and higher than a kite. We climbed back across the broken ground to the fence and were relieved to find he just wanted to tell us we were on private property and would have to find another beach. We drove off so shook-up that they decided to go straight to Fullerton that evening and then head for San Diego the next morning.

The people in Fullerton had a little house right across the street from the University — probably one of the drug outlets for the campus. We sat around and talked and smoked dope and fell asleep on the floor. The next morning we started out for San Diego, and before noon we were over the cliffs searching through the caves and along the many little beaches of that dynamic coastline.

Mike, the one in charge of the THC and the apparent leader of the gang, was a Viet Nam veteran with a weird wound on his arm, and around his shoulder and chest. His face was partly held together by plastic surgery, making him look slightly frightening and yet pitiful. He called the shots most of the time, and I figured he was the owner of the Golden Edsel.

He went off hunting abalone shells alone, while Jim – the dark-headed farmer's son whom I had met in SPD – sat on a large rock watching the tide break against the rugged shore.

The cliffs behind us were nearly a hundred feet high, massive bulwarks standing against the pounding surf. I climbed across the rocky tide-pools to where Jim was sitting. The bright cool air was charged with the fragrance of salt and kelp. We sat in silence reveling in the sunshine.

About a half a mile to the south stood a point of land far out into the waves, hiding the rugged coast as it wound its way toward the Mexican border. Jim dreamed, "Wouldn't you love to just start out walking around that point and never come back?"

"Do you really mean it?" I asked.

Jim looked at me for a moment. His eyes seemed to strain for my soul. "Well. . . I guess," he said. "I mean it's so beautiful. I'd like to live out here forever."

"Let's do it," I said.

He looked away from the point and back into my face, "You mean it, don't you?"

Of course I meant it, I was a pioneer in life's wilderness. I was so out of it I thought I could just walk away and live off the land by faith. "Let's go," I said. I looked at the point of land. White water splashed high against the cliffs. I looked into Jim's eyes earnestly, ready to go. About that time Mike came across the rocks carrying a gunny sack heavy with abalone shells.

That afternoon we traded some THC for food at Taco Bell and started back toward Fullerton. We were flying high and wild. It was our big joke (and we about half believed it) that the Golden Edsel could drive herself. But we were suddenly sobered when she drove us right up into a police roadblock. I was dissatisfied with the way Mike was handling the officer, so I leaned over and looked out myself. I knew I was the cleanest cut one of the bunch and thought if he got a look at me with my fairly short hair, he might not hassle us too much. I also had my ID all squared away, even down to my old Student Union Card from Long Beach State; when all else failed, I knew I could pass as a student and get by almost anything. He sent us on our way.

That night in Fullerton, a large crowd gathered. I was drinking coffee and trying to get my head straightened out. Around midnight a number of them started taking cocaine. Along about two in the morning the place was littered with sleeping bodies. I kept a close watch on the clock in the kitchen. I knew we had to leave by four a.m. if I was going to get to work by six.

At four o'clock I tried to stir Jim and Mike. They were not easy to wake. When they finally did come around, they were so drugged they could hardly stand up. Mike never even tried, he just lay there with his head propped on one elbow looking like a zombie.

"We're going to have to get going pretty quick," I said. "It's about four o'clock and it'll take almost two hours to get to Long Beach."

They looked at me like I was insane. "Man," Jim blinked, "we can't get you home, we're too stoned."

"You promised to get me back this morning."

"Man. . ." he labored, "we're too loaded, Brad."

"Work's a phoney trip," Mike added. "You don't need it, man."

"Come on," I said flatly, "I've got to be there at six o'clock."

"Forget it, Brad," Jim said, "you don't need to go to work."

Mike yawned, "Right. . . Don't let it bother you, man. Just stay high. Work's a phoney trip, man, you don't need it."

"Look, you guys said. . ." But I could see it was no use. Jim was already lying back in the big chair and Mike was rolling over on the floor.

Jim was making himself comfortable with a pillow he had gotten off the couch, "Hey, Brad, turn off the light, will you? Don't worry about it, man," he finished in his sleepy voice. "Get some sleep, man."

I sat on the couch in the dark thinking about the miles between me and the Edgewater Inn. The floor was covered with sleepers and heavy breathing. The clock in the kitchen ticked off the time in slow minutes. Friends! With friends like these I was more than alone, I was in the midst of a herd of stupid cattle. Finally the windows turned grey and I stepped into the kitchen to see what time it was. Five-fifteen. I went back to the couch.

It was light enough now that I could see the sleepers clearly. There lay Jim, my old Army buddy. We had had some

86

good times ditching work details together, but really he was as much a stranger to me as any of the others. And then there was Mike, kind of a spiritualist with ugly scars. He had these people wrapped around his little finger and was soaking their very lives away. He was the boss, the freak's freak, the demonic leader. Then there were the rest of the people lying around on the floors and chairs and off in the bedrooms.

The day was about to dawn when I made another trip to the kitchen clock. Five minutes to six. In five minutes I was supposed to be walking through the big glass doors of the Edgewater Inn. Out the kitchen window the sky above the backyard was blue. Under the big tree was a jumble of boards and junk. There was an old wrecked car, wet with dew, turning to rust. The day was just beginning. I watched the seconds tick off before six o'clock, and as the second hand moved passed the twelve, I became the only person in the world. The kitchen was a nasty mess, garbage stood around on the floor by the full trash can.

I made my way back through the bodies and quietly passed through the front door and onto the porch. The grass on the college lawns across the street glittered with dew under a sky that was hollow and early. Red sunlight was striking the tops of the buildings. I walked out to the sidewalk. The neighborhood was silent. East, up the street, the sun was a ball of fire standing above a purple mountain range.

I looked back at the house. Far away in Long Beach, the Edgewater Inn was waking up. They were wondering what was keeping me.

I walked toward the rising sun. As it turned yellow and then white and moved off toward the south, I moved with it, down the sidewalks and across the streets. Bitterness ate away at my spirit as I trudged angrily along.

I held my course obstinately to the direction of the climbing sun until it led me up an exit of some freeway and left me standing in the traffic, confused. The sun was moving south with an iron will, but my way had been blocked. Cars whizzed past in the morning rush. Far to the east and across miles of city, a mountain range stood out clearly against the sky. Somewhere up in those mountains I had once been to a state park, and it struck my mind to go up there instead of following the sun.

87

I had already been talking to God about my so-called friends, my job, and my bitterness. I had told Him I was through trying to live any longer. I was finished. Done. Now I told Him I was going to walk up to Irvine Park, and there He would either tell me things that would quiet my soul and direct my life, or I would lie down and die.

I walked for nine solid hours. All day I talked with God and all day He listened. "I'm sick of living. I can't go on another day." I was in earnest, my heart was splitting. "I'm going up to that park and I'm going to talk to Jesus Christ."

I was out of my mind? Yes. And, I was as serious as death can make a man. "You'll have to be there, Jesus. You've got to talk with me in the open." I made an appointment to see Jesus that day. I was determined I would walk up under a Douglas fir somewhere in those mountains and either Jesus would be standing there in white robe and sandaled feet, or else He would come walking out of the woods to meet me. It was an appointment I intended to keep, and I believed enough in the integrity of God to feel that He would either meet me there or compromise His existence.

It was a long hot walk. My sandals gathered dust which turned to mud between my toes. I had on a khaki shirt and a pair of jeans, and I did not have a penny to my name except for one I found on the street. By now I had three days' growth of whiskers and must have looked pretty scruffy. I was walking through a nice neighborhood when a squad car pulled up behind me and honked; somebody must have called in about the rough-looking character walking down their middle-class sidewalk. There were times when all I was able to do was keep a straight face and say, "Yes, Sir" while showing my driver's license and college identification. As long as a guy was in college, he could look as scruffy as he wanted and it was as American as apple pie.

I got a drink at a gas station before I started up the first foothill leading into the park. The afternoon was hot and I was tremendously weary. As I topped the first hill, to my dismay, the road quit abruptly and out across the little valley and up over the next ridge, there was a huge four-lane highway under construction. Road graders were groaning behind walls of dirt and big dump-trucks were on the move up and down the mountain. I approached a Spanish man who was standing behind a water truck and asked how I could get into the park. He said the road was closed and the only way I could possibly get in would be directly over the ridge. That might have been a disappointment for anyone else, but for me it was a monumental dilemma. I had an appointment to see Jesus Christ up there and I had to get in.

The steep ridge was covered with needle-sharp cactus and volcanic stones, and I was too exhausted to try it. There had to be a better way. I walked back over to the side of the last hill so I could survey the situation. The cactus-covered ridge was too high and too difficult. The construction site was out of question — too much going on and too many people to tell me to get off. It looked impossible. I started to cry. Then I prayed for help. I was almost there. How could I quit now? Where would I go? This was the end of the road. There was no place to turn. I wished with all my heart that I could die.

I was sitting sobbing when I heard the rocks. My hungry soul was so ravished with sin, famishing with hunger, until suddenly the very rocks on the hillside cried out. "Storm the gates of strife!" they wailed. "Force your passage through!"

I took courage. I started right up through the construction zone. When I got onto the elevated grade, I spotted a steep trail where dirt bikes had been ridden through the brush beside the fresh soil of the roadbed. I crossed the mound of earth that separated the construction from the desert and started up through the brush. Barbed wire had been torn down for the road and was curled up in a tangle across my way. I leaped and caught the top of my foot making a painful gash. Then I had to crawl under a scratchy mesquite tree. It was not much of a trail, but it was better than the cactus ridge. I noticed blood on my muddy feet and was reminded of the sandaled foot of the One with Whom I was to meet in just a few minutes. I could see His dusty feet bearing a heavy cross up Calvary. I felt His presence and I began to bawl. Through tears of grief and despair I struggled up the mountain, weary beyond measure. "I'm coming! I'm coming!" I cried, my head swimming in the California heat. "Oh, God, I'll be there in a minute!"

The construction went on through the gap which it had created between two rocky points. I trudged up to the high point on the left, hoping to find a way over. The top was flat, covered with stones and desert dust. East, in the direction of the park, all I could see was a densely forested valley and a high pine-covered ridge. Beyond that was another ridge, then another and another. To the north, it was the same. But way down in the southern end of a hidden valley, like a beacon sticking up out of the forest, I saw a white steeple. With an exhausted scream of despair I cried, "I can't make it!" and fell down on my hands and knees. I cried until I had no cry left in me. I couldn't make it. Tears were drying on my face. I wiped my nose on my bare wrist. My hands were sweaty and muddy.

With head hanging limp from tired shoulders, I was at the end of life's journey. Existence no longer had meaning. There was nothing to hope for but audience with my Maker, and He was not there.

They say that if a person will lie perfectly still for a fair amount of time in an area where there are buzzards, it will not be long before one will begin to investigate. It is even said that a buzzard will land and begin to peck at a living being if lying perfectly still. I looked up into the sky to petition the mercy of God. There hung a red-headed California condor, wings spread on the atmosphere, black and foreboding against the hot sky.

Along with the penny I had picked up, I had collected four other items: a smooth rock, half a black-walnut shell, a dead seedpod, and a hard red berry. Each represented a person. I was the stone. I pulled them all out of my pocket and held them in my hand. The buzzard was making hard circles about thirty feet above me as I laid my treasures in the dust. "Here," I said. "This is all I've got."

I was solemn. Empty. There was a burden on my shoulders as big as the world, and the shadow of a buzzard on my soul. I got up from where I had been kneeling and walked slowly back to the edge of the peak. I started down the rocky path. I had absolutely no place to go. Jesus was supposed to have met me there. When I got a few yards down the path I looked back, thinking He might have appeared while my back was turned. The buzzard was just landing on my sacrifice.

At that moment something happened to me that had never happened before in my life. "It is enough," God must have said. "There is a young man on a dusty California hilltop who cannot go another moment without hearing from heaven." And out of the empty sky He unloaded a chariot full of glory over my soul. Jesus kept the appointment. On that dusty hill near Irvine Park, He laid His wonderful hands on my head, and down through my entire being poured hope and faith and heavenly satisfaction. "I AM," said He. "I am God. I am listening, Brad, and I care."

I started down the hill and I knew God was looking right at me. He had kept the appointment in His own way. I came away no less impressed than if Jesus Christ had in fact come walking up in a white robe and sandaled feet and spoken words of peace to my famishing spirit.

When I got down to where they were cutting the highway through the gap, instead of starting down the side-path, I struck right out into the middle of the road where there was a mound of fresh dirt running the length of the grade all the way to the bottom. A pickup truck came rolling down behind me and stopped and the man waved me over to him. I was expecting a reprimand, but was greeted instead by a smile and an invitation to ride down in his truck. When the man smiled, I saw the love of Christ in his face — and God revealed to me that Jesus was not walking around in sandaled feet, but was living in men. Divine love embraced me as we talked, and I'll always believe that that man knew God. He let me out just across the road from a gas station where there was a drinking fountain, and he smiled and waved.

> The first day I met Jesus
> He was a truck-driving man
> Building highways for my journeys,
> reaching out to the horizon.
> At first I said to Jesus,
> Aren't you tired my good man
> And with a smile as big as gold,
> Not till this road is done.
> I knew I could not pass Him
> lest the road I used was His
> And as He drove me back to my streets
> I saw the way He paved for men.
> I asked Him if this road He builds
> gets Him closer to the end

He smiled again, the end was His
and so my road began.
He pointed me to water
as I stepped down from His truck
And back to where the dawn began
my day of walking up.

I was sitting on the curb resting and had no idea where I was going when a couple of girls pulled up and offered me a ride. I really was not hitch-hiking but I said yes, deciding I'd just go where they were going and worry about the next step later. I had told God as I started down the hill that I did not know what to do or where to go, but that I'd just take one step at a time and trust Him to work out the details.

The girls said they were going down into Fullerton and I said I'd ride all the way with them. I must have looked and smelled a sight. They asked me where I was from and I silently pointed back up into the mountain. They dropped me off not too far from the college, which I interpreted as God's leadership, and found my way to the little house across the street from the campus.

The next day when Jim and Mike started toward northern California in the Golden Edsel, I was in the back seat. Mike traded some THC for gasoline and we moved up the highway right past the Edgewater Inn, and the "WELCOME GREAT PUMPKIN" sign, which I had put up there in some other lifetime. Then it was north through Los Angeles, Santa Barbara, San Luis Obispo, Salinas. The entire day and night were a jumble of hitchhikers, stops to visit strange people (probably to sell THC), and long hours on the highway. We headed into San Francisco in the wee hours, drove through the deserted city, across the Golden Gate Bridge and into Sausalito. There Mike found the house of a friend of his where the three of us laid out on the living room floor to sleep.

The next day we went back into San Francisco to one of those tall, straight, old Victorian houses where some of the heaviest freaks I'd ever been with were having a hashish party. We had been there about an hour when everybody began leaving and I started wondering what my next step should be, to go with Mike and Jim, or just stay where I was? The guy who lived there was sitting in a corner stringing a guitar and I sat down beside him to watch. After a few minutes he looked up and said, "You'd better hurry up, they're going to leave and you'll miss the party." I took this to be direction from above and moved seriously on, climbing into the Golden Edsel just as it was pulling away from the curb.

We drove up into the forests of northern California that afternoon, making a few more stops to sell dope. By evening we were at a huge Halloween bash thrown by some people on a mountain farm. Most of the San Francisco freaks I had met that afternoon were there, plus a lot more I had never seen before. I had forgotten all about it being Halloween until I saw the costumes. In fact, it didn't sink in until I'd been there a couple of hours that they were costumes. For all I knew, the guy in the herringbone knickers and climbing boots was fresh off the European mountainside, and the girl in the gown carrying the molded candle in a macramé sling was out of a real fairy tale up in the forest.

The night was full of confusion. Morning light found me wide awake and in a state of fear and desolation. I did not know where I was. I did not know who I was with, what day it was, or where I was going. Jim found me wandering around outside farmhouse and things began to make a little more sense.

§§§

Late that night we pulled into Jim's hometown, Corcoran, just sixty miles north of Bakersfield. We woke a friend of his who gave us a bed for the night. When Jim called his folks the next morning to let them know he was back in town, there was a message for me to call home. I had left a note on my table back in Long Beach in case somebody had wanted to know where I was on my days off. The note mentioned Jim's name. Since my parents knew of only one Jim, they had phoned his parents when I turned up missing.

It was about ten thirty that morning when I called collect from a pay phone. I had been missing for six days and Mom was worried sick. Knowing I was probably on drugs, she was very careful over the phone. She just casually asked, since I was so close, why didn't I come home for a while. It was like coaxing an endangered child away from a cliff without running up and scaring him over the edge, she was very tactful. I said I would probably come home that day, but couldn't say for sure. There was no pattern or plan to my goings, I was simply taking the turns as they came in the path.

Mike had been lecturing Jim all week on the evils of the establishment and materialism, and had finally worked his logic around to the subject of the Golden Edsel. It turned out that the Edsel was Jim's all the time. That morning Mike finally worked on Jim's mind until Jim gave him the Edsel for nearly nothing and counted it a blessing to be loosed from such a worldly fetter.

Mike was a real con-man, a crook from way back; but he had a way about him, some spiritual influence that got a hold on people. He may have been demon possessed. He was definitely involved in some sort of spiritualism, but he never could make me understand it, and before he had known me twenty-four hours, he had given up trying.

Mike cleaned up the old Edsel that morning and was heading back for northern California alone when I decided to pack along. He was kind of surprised but said it would be all right. I figured since a ride had not appeared to take me to Bakersfield, then this must be the next move.

When we got out to Highway 99, he stopped for gas. He presented a credit card and things got tense. The man was afraid to take it. We must have looked rough. I had not bathed, shaved, or changed clothes for a week; I was wild-eyed, crazy, and as touchy as a rat in a cross fire. Then there was Mike, scar-faced, long scraggly hair — a real freaky-looking character. Anyway, the man decided not to take the credit card, and a regular argument ensued. Finally the man agreed to leave the station with his hired help and take Mike into Tulare to check out the card.

I sat alone in the Golden Edsel for about five minutes. Something told me that card was stolen and I got scared. "I'm not going to follow a thief around California."

I told the Golden Edsel goodbye, walked out to the highway, and caught a ride to Bakersfield. It was about four o'clock in the afternoon when I called Mom from a restaurant on the outskirts of town, and she came and picked me up. Never once did I doubt her love for me. She was kind and long-suffering through all my troubled years of dope and insanity, although she never compromised her hatred and opposition for the things I was involved in. Only now as I look back, can I even get a glimpse of what grief she must have experienced in her heart.

Chapter Nine

BURT'S BASEMENT

It is the first week in November, 1970. I'm twenty-three years old but I'm not. I am a poor sick child. Don't feel sorry for me. It's my own fault. I ought to be out there making a living and raising a family; but I am a mental, emotional, and spiritual mess. I am helpless — a social invalid — and I finally realize it. As I sit watching my mother cook supper, I am compelled to pour my heart out, but I don't know where to start.

"Mom," I say (I haven't been this humble before her in years), "I need help."

"I know it, Honey," she says. She puts down her dishcloth and looks at me with eyes full of pity and confusion, "I want you to have just what you need. I just wish I knew what I could do."

"I know, Mom," I'm looking down at the table. "I know you're doing all you can. I don't know what's wrong with me." I glance at her. She is standing at the sink looking at me. I know she loves me. "I'm just lost," I say. "It seems like. . . I don't know. . . I don't know what to do or where to go."

She turns and looks out the window, "I have an idea." I feel sorry for her. I know she doesn't want to push anything on me and it's easy to follow her lead, "What is it?"

She told me she had heard of a Christian youth worker she thought would be willing to meet me. It sounded like a lame possibility, but wanting to make her happy, I said I'd try it.

In a couple of days she had made an appointment for me to go with this guy named Ron to a cross-country track meet. At the appointed time he honked and I climbed in beside him. Ron was thirty-fivish, clean-cut, and nice — a perfect "Christian Youth Worker of America" type.

During the next two months I was involved in sports, College Bible club, cottage prayer groups, and a retreat to Mount Hermon for college students. I wasn't a college student anymore, but that was about my age group, and that was the group Ron was the leader of. I had not hung around them very long before I thought I was a Christian. I was simply becoming one of them socially and that was the only way I could see that there was any difference between them and anyone else: they hung around together.

Mount Hermon is a Christian conference grounds located in the Santa Cruz area. It was situated right up in the densely forested area between Felton and Scott's Valley. There was preaching and lectures, food and fellowship, beautiful buildings and natural surroundings. The things that impressed me most were the mountains, the redwoods, and the town of Santa Cruz. The deep of my soul was never reached during that retreat. I did not need a retreat, I needed a reality.

I don't know how much Ron and company knew about the things I needed, but there were some people in Santa Cruz who knew. There were some people by the name of Walrath just a few miles away who had by now seen their home overrun by young people seeking and finding God. Beverly's kitchen cupboards and bedroom closets were no longer her own. Her family heirlooms and valuable keepsakes had been grabbed off the shelves by wandering vagabonds who had no more respect for them than for Dixie Cups and paper towels. Things she had loved and saved through the years were broken or lost or had simply disappeared. The little two-bedroom house seemed to be falling apart at the seams, and Wally was spending every available hour repairing and reinforcing the structure and utilities

§§§

I was working for my Dad at the Buttonwillow cotton gin, trying to make a little money and trying to keep my head straight. I grew tired of the Christian Youth thing and started making plans to go back to Toronto. Jill and I had been corresponding right along and the only direction I could find in life seemed to center around her.

That Christmas, just before I left for Canada, Mom bought me a nice black-leather Bible and wrote in the presentation page, "To my son, the new Christian, forever, Mom." I also thought I was a Christian. I had even started wearing a turquoise and silver Navajo cross around my neck.

My first week in Toronto I spent at Jill's parents' home, and the first Sunday we all went to church together. I was starting to feel almost righteous.

It was only a matter of days before I realized that my relationship with Jill had gone stale. Suddenly I found myself thousands of miles from home, and my only purpose for being there was quickly fading into a nightmare. I grew sick and bitter. Jill and I seemed to do nothing but argue hatefully. By the end of two weeks, I was trying to figure out how to get away from her.

Jill's best friend was Nancy, and Nancy went with a guy named Bob Adam. He and I got along very well and decided to share an apartment together. We found a place down in Mimico on Lake Shore Drive. We put a couple of pictures of Jesus on the wall and I got a parakeet which we named "Jesus Sky Pilot," and hung his cage from the ceiling in the center of the living room. The Bible from Mom was put with my never-used things and forgotten.

Bob was a sales representative and repairman for Pitney-Bowes Business Machines. He was a humble, honest sort of guy and we got along like close brothers from the beginning.

Those winter months spent in Toronto may be better told through my poetry. I had a little cot where I slept before the old double windows of the bedroom. There I would sit by the hour and write and daydream and pray, and look out at the snow and trees and Lake Ontario.

> I'm lost and I'm proud
> and not much right comes from my walk
> and I'm a child no more
> a man now walking on to find Jesus Christ
> or whoever else is still alive

§§§

> on this paper I scratch desperately
> and on a door somewhere You hear my scratch
> do You figure it's the wind
> don't You know I need in
> won't You just trip Your latch
> won't You please let me in

§§§

I would like to know what makes the seasons run
from the heat and from the cold
then I might know what makes me run
from the young and from the old
What keeps me tight
running from the day and hiding from the night
like sparrow's flight
I never stop
from north to south

§§§

I have friends but I am lonely
my heart bends but love is only
disappearing
grasp at hope and watch it vanish
grasp at death but morning always comes
who wills this no-one state I'm in
who will come and stop the spin I'm in
what will end this endless hell I'm in

§§§

twenty-five cents and four dollars
that's it
no home
no life
no future
nothing I want
to do
or see
or feel
or be
nothing

§§§

I don't want much
just for God to sit next to me on my bed

so that I can see Him
just like that
and hold my hand
and make it all better

§§§

everybody's smiling photo at the wall across
the room
everybody slapping backs and ho-hoing hugging
a friend
everybody seems to know where it's at
everybody's nowhere but me
I'm alone
somewhere
nothing to do
no place to go
life is a stallion
running free without

§§§

walking like always toward some light
I trip on something and everywhere are stickers
in my hands
so I sit there guessing God will give me some
bliss
or something
not asking Him a lot of questions He's tired of
because I know He is really out there
and knows me
I was so lonely I looked to Him
my cat ran away and never came back
amen

§§§

trees point like skeletons up into the sky
their arms make patterns change throughout the wind

there are clouds above the lake to ride that wind
one dollar in my pocket wonders why
if snow can ride the wind than why can't I

in winter jobless sparrows fly about
they ride the patterns changing through the limbs
they whistle through those faithful little grins
they know quite well their God and winter ends
if birds can last till spring then why can't I

greyness in the cloud begins to toll
limbs are silhouetted against the cold
sparrows fly up underneath the eaves
snow now whispers round like falling leaves
another day has past and I feel old

I found a job which lasted three weeks, helping set up a new bookstore. Bob started teaching me to play the guitar, and with plenty of time on my hands and plenty of creative energy to use up, I started writing songs. Nature was generally the theme, as that was where I could see the greatest evidences of the Creator. Those were terribly hungry days for my soul. Not a hour passed when I didn't pull heaven's bell rope in one way or another.

I had never put any stock in dreams, but one lonely night I passed through a situation that left such an impression that it has never been forgotten. What brought me into the dream was the jingle of bells as I walked through the front door of a little shop which sold baskets, kettles, and incense, brass buttons, weavings, and tea. There was no one there, and as I was browsing through, I happened upon another door which led off the selling floor. I entered and found myself in a country kitchen where a young mother was preparing lunch for her husband and children. I walked over to the back door and looked out through the screen across magnificent rolling fields of orchards and green produce. Then I sat down at their table and started playing my tambourine. I played loud and hard and was surprised when I wasn't told to shut up. In fact they seemed to be enjoying it when all of a sudden, I sensed I was waking.

I looked at the young man, "Please keep me here."

He smiled, "No one is kept here."

"You must get here on your own," added the mother. "Then you can stay forever."

"Leave behind the things you must," the man said, clearly encouraging me to make the trip.

They were fading from my consciousness and I reached out, yearning for them to hold me. The last instruction I heard was "Travel light, it's not a short walk." And with that I awoke into my room.

I never could forget that dream, it seemed to speak of heaven and eternal life. I always felt as if it had been sent to encourage me in my search for truth and reality.

That winter I met a guy named Burt who lived in a basement under a big old red brick house about a half mile from Bob and me. He had a good stereo and a stack of records that seemed to have no end.

I was at Burt's one night during a March blizzard when I was introduced to Mickey. He came blowing in with the snow all over him, like something out of the Northwest Territory. He'd walked two miles through the storm and was brimming with good cheer and charisma. I was the new guy and a stranger. There was not a lot said between us until he started talking about a trip he was planning to West Virginia the following week. I don't remember what I said or how, but by the time we left Burt's that night, Mickey and I were pretty well acquainted and I was in for the trip.

On our way down through the States we ended up with a hitchhiker from the University of Gettysburg who was on his way home for the weekend to Newport News, Virginia. I knew something about Newport News from my AWOL days and so the friendship began. We took him all the way home, had a shower at his parents' house, and then he took us out on the town. His name was Johnny, but his friends all called him "Greek" because of his nationality. And friends he had aplenty. We had only been in town a few hours when we were involved with a great number of locals, most of whom were raised with a lot of money and freedom and knew how to show a bunch of Canadians a good time.

The second evening we were sitting around a campfire on the shores of Chesapeake Bay listening to some local folk singers when I had a brainstorm. I kicked back and thought it over while

102

the music and conversation drifted on without me. The money I had made working at the bookstore was quickly running out. I had been waiting for the weather to moderate before leaving Toronto. As the fire burned and the singers sang, it made more and more sense to just keep on going south now, since I was this far already. It was almost springtime in Virginia, and no doubt it was spring in the south. Then and there I decided I would head for Florida the next morning when Mickey and the guys started back north.

"Hey, Mickey," I said under the volume of the conversation. He leaned over. "Hey, listen," I began, "you're going home tomorrow aren't you?"

"Yeah," he said. "Why?"

"I hope you don't mind, but I don't think I'll be going."

"What do you mean? What are you going to do?"

"I think I'm going to go to Florida."

"What?" he said. "When?"

"In the morning, I guess. I really haven't planned it very far. I'm not sure where I'll go first."

"You mean you're going to just up and go to Florida? Just like that?" he was incredulous.

"Yeah, I guess," I grinned. "I was getting ready to leave Toronto pretty soon anyhow. It might as well be now as ever." I looked back at the fire taking a conscious breath of the fertile breeze. "Man, it's warm here; it's bound to be even warmer in Florida. I've got some of my things with me and, well, I don't know." He was looking at me like I was a circus freak. "Well, anyway, I think I'm going to take off tomorrow."

Mickey looked at the fire and then back to me. "You're kidding."

"No."

After a moment he got up and walked down by the water. Overhead the sky was navy blue, and on the horizon it was blood red through black clouds. The waters of Chesapeake Bay were at peace. I walked out to where he was standing. We could hear the singers and the fire behind us. "Do you really mean it" he said with his hands stuck down in his pockets.

"Yeah. I mean it," I chuckled. "Why?"

"Well, I don't know," he said, "I just never knew anybody who would just strike out like that. Right out into nowhere, I mean."

"Oh, I guess I'll eventually get back to California," I said.

"Yeah, but, just like that!" The sky was darkening, frogs and crickets sang noisily in the cool night air. We stood for a few minutes enjoying the silence and I was about to go back to the fire when Mickey broke in again. "Listen," he said, "if you'll go with me back to Toronto long enough for me to sell my car and get a van, we'll go together."

"To Florida?" I said.

"Yeah."

"Really?"

"Yeah, really," he grinned. "I've been wanting to do something like this for a long time but I never had anyone to go with. I'm ready! We'll go all the way to California together."

"Well," I thought aloud, "how long will it take before we leave?" I'd been dying to get going for a month, now that I had my mind made up I wasn't interested in any delays.

"I promise we'll be gone by the first of April," he was in earnest. "What do you say?"

"OK. Sounds good." I looked at him. "You really mean it, now?"

"I'll give two weeks' notice Tuesday at work, and start selling my car immediately."

"OK," I said. "Great."

§§§

It took Mickey right up until April first to get ready. In the meantime, one night in Burt's basement with my back against the TV listening to his stereo, I was gripped by the words of one of the songs. The tune was kind of country-rock, and went like this:

"One day up in heaven, all the heavenly host was gathered there
Satan was among them
Satan went to God, and God said, Satan, where have you been
Satan said, I've been on earth, among men
God said, You must have seen my faithful servant Job
You must have seen his worth, and how he's evil's foe
Yes, Job is evil's foe

Satan said, Well, yes, God, Job is your man
But what if You struck him God, what would he do then
He'd turn his back on You and curse Your name right to Your face
God said, all right Bub, go and test his faith
Just go and try Job's faith.

Oh my God, Oh my God, cried poor Job
I have lost everything I owned,
I lost my cattle, I lost my land, You took my children, too
I'm losing my mind and the love of my wife
But I still have faith in You
Oh my God, Oh my God, can't You hear poor Job
This world can no longer be my home
My so-called friends speak biting words, telling me what to do
My health is gone, I cannot rest
But I keep my faith in You — so
There we see poor Job, down in the ashes of his burned-out farm
Seven days and seven nights they watched him there
'Til finally one said, Oh, Job
What evil have you done to bring God's wrath upon you?
And about that time down the road comes Elihu.
That young man lectured Job, til Job's poor heart near broke
Then from the whirling wind, God Himself spoke, He said
Who are these who claim to know my workings and all my ways
Job has proved his faith and shall live joyous days
And Job lived joyous days"

I had to hear it again, it was written for me. "Hey, Burt!"

He came out of his stupor and looked over dreamily, "Yeah?"

"Could I listen to that song again?"

"What?" he shouted over the music.

"I want to listen to that song again!" I yelled. "What song?"

"That one about Job."

"Why?"

"I just want to hear it again," I shouted. "Can I put it back?"

"Sure, go ahead. But I don't get it. Why that song?"

"Listen," I said as I put the needle gently back, "it's about faith, and God."

"So what," Burt laughed, and the rest of the guys in Burt's basement chimed in. They had been interrupted from their reveries and thought I was a bit of a quack.

"What is faith?" someone asked Burt, clearly teasing me.

"I don't know," he smirked. "It's like when you don't have anything you can still have faith." They all laughed.

I laughed right along with them. It never bothered me to be the joke. I was the foreigner from California and was used to getting teased by them. They were what I called "city guys": dress shoes, shiny shirts, hairdos, hot cars. I was the "country boy from out west" with my boots, accent, and no haircut at all. But this time I knew it was no joke, for I was the guy who didn't have anything. I knew there was a God. And I believed that my faith would one day bring me to Him. The song for Job made me feel a lot better, and my faith was strengthened.

As I got more closely acquainted with Mickey, I was introduced to his family. His father was a preacher; the first day I walked into their kitchen, he greeted me with a warm handshake and a hearty, "God bless you." There was a difference in that home. Mickey's mother and two teenaged sisters wore modest, old-fashioned dresses, and the girls had very long hair hanging down their backs. All three were working at the housework in a harmony I didn't know existed between mothers and daughters anymore. I learned later that Mickey's father preached in the Russian language to Russian-speaking people in Toronto.

Mickey (who's true Russian name was Miodrog) bought a white Ford van and we prepared it for the trip by putting carpets on the floors and walls and some large pillows for comfort. It had been some sort of company truck of some sort, and on the dashboard were the letters S-O-2. All we could figure was Sulfur Dioxide, but what in the world was that? Anyway we called her the SO2 and started down the highway on the first of April.

Chapter Ten

BEING

Mickey introduced me to Brent just days before we left Toronto. Brent had decided to go with us to Florida because he was in a big fight with his girl-friend and wanted to get away from town for a while. I didn't care much for the guy, but it didn't really matter to me if he went along.

Our first step was Gettysburg, where we picked up Greek and a friend of his who were going with us to Fort Lauderdale for Easter Week. While Greek took his last exam at the university, "Montana," his friend, showed us around the Gettysburg battlefields. Then we were on the road south.

Ft. Lauderdale was a jumble of rock bands, crowds of people from sidewalk to sidewalk, police, and chaos. I was wanting to get out alone and enjoy the beautiful Florida scenery, but every beach was packed with mobs of young people. It was a great social event, of course, when all the youth from all around gathered for a week of reveling. To me it was just another crazy scene to try to cope with. I was glad to be out on the high road with nothing to do but enjoy every day to the hilt, but as far as I was concerned enjoyment was a solitary setting with the mighty workings of nature manifesting themselves.

I was standing on the water's edge that second evening letting the waves wash up around my ankles. A band was playing up the beach and most of the hordes were there. The sky was a translucent mixture of aqua and pink and the Atlantic horizon was growing darker and darker. The evening star, probably Venus, was standing with the half-moon in an empty sky. The little waves were breaking eternally against the sand and I was alone. I looked at my watch.

Why in the world did I look at my watch? I didn't care any more about the time than I did the stock index. As I looked out on the darkening Atlantic, I was fingering a piece of sea shell I had in my pocket. I pulled it out. It was just over an inch across, a broken piece of a much larger shell smoothed by years in the tide. It had two little fin-like structures standing up on its brown back. I looked at my watch again, not the time, just the watch. Then I laid the shell over it, as if in its place. One fin for day, I thought, and one for night.

I undid the watch from the leather band which was just wider than the watch itself. Then I put the band back together with the shell in its place. It was perfect. The smaller strap fit between the two fins holding it securely to the larger leather band. I put it back on my wrist. "One for day, and one for night," I said out loud. "That's all the time I need to know, and all I care about." And I skipped the watch out into the waves.

"If birds can just be birds," I said, "and if deer can just be deer; if earth can just be earth, and the sea sea, then I can I not just be me?"

Why couldn't a man just live, just be? Why worry and plan and build and destroy? Why be a businessman or a lawyer or an architect or an anything? Why not just be a man? A human? "That's right," I chuckled. "I'm a human being being human."

§§§

The third day in "Ft. Peopledale" was our last, to my great joy. Greek and Montana had found a ride north with some other college students. About half the crowds were still milling around hoping for another night of craziness as we pulled out toward the Everglades. The day was hot. We crossed Florida through swamps and jungles on Highway 41. That afternoon we spent some time on the first Gulf beach we came to in Naples, and later found a spot a few miles up the coast where we spent the night in the van.

We had decided to spend the next day there and were enjoying the beautiful morning when we met some kids from Gainesville who were camping down the same stretch of beach. I spent most of the day alone in the timber and the surf. That evening we ate with them and spent another night in the van.

The next day we drove up to Cedar Key where we spent some time hiking through the jungles and across the white sands. There we ran into yet another guy from Gainesville named Mark, who was out for an afternoon motorcycle ride. As evening came on, the four of us were in a little cafe on the pier having supper. About halfway through the meal we got talking with a couple of shrimpers who ran a boat off the Gulf Coast. They seemed to take a liking to us and wanted to treat us to a beer. They were rough and not much to be trusted, but we figured we'd let them buy us a beer anyway. We followed them to their favorite tavern.

It was dark outside the bar, and it was darker inside. I was sitting in a booth with one of the shrimpers called Quickdraw getting chummier all the time. Brent went to get something out of the van. I never noticed that he hadn't come back, until I realized Mickey and Mark had gone outside as well.

I had just ordered another glass, and was wondering where they had all gone off to, when Mickey appeared. He stepped over to where I was sitting and said, "Hey, Brad, come here just a minute. . ."

I followed him out onto the sidewalk, a bit confused.

"Come on!!" he said, and took off running across the street.

I trotted over to the van. When I came around the side, Brent jumped in the side door, pulling me in after him — "Man that was slick!!" He slammed the door shut. "I was sure we'd never get you out of there!"

The van lurched forward. Mickey sped down the street. Mark's motorcycle was inside the van. We went zooming out of town as they told me the story. When Brent went out of the bar earlier, a city cop who was half drunk told him that those shrimpers were some pretty bad guys, and were probably setting us up for a rotten deal. He said we'd better get away from them and out of town as quickly as possible. Brent had gotten the news to Mickey and Mark, but they didn't know how to get me away from Quickdraw. They knew the other shrimper would soon get suspicious if they kept hanging around the door whispering.

Now we were anxious about them starting after us in their car. But they never appeared, and it wasn't long before we were far down the road and feeling happy.

It was already been determined that we were going to Gainesville to be with the people we had met on the beach the day before; so we drove Mark and his bike home and spent the night on his floor.

Mark had a job in a little store that sold and traded stereo tapes. Between there and his house, and the house of a girl named Wendy whom we had met in Naples, we kept pretty busy.

One night a bunch of us were sitting around doing some

weird kind of Eastern thing with special cards when Brent sprang the news that he was going back to Toronto the next day. It was a shock, but to me it was not a disappointment. We drove him to the Tampa airport the next day and that was that. He had said his mother was sick and had asked him to return; but Mickey, who knew him a lot better than I, figured he had made up with his girlfriend over the phone and she had put the pressure on.

Florida was fantastic. Every day at three o'clock it rained, but raining or not, the weather was drenching all the time. It was a beautiful jungle and a hot steamy rain forest. The insects and weeds were out of another age; it was like walking back in time, to a place where nature ruled with the power of the fittest. This was not in the unpopulated areas only — thick turf and rank leaves covered every inch that was not paved. The bugs were outrageous, but they seemed to be accepted as a way of life by the people who lived there.

One night after a set with Mark's massive stereo system, we were sitting around talking about the road and our destinations when Mickey and I both got a powerful urge to hit the highway. It was two o'clock in the morning, but we had road fever so bad that we just threw everything in the van and took off into the night. Mark was shocked by our sudden departure, but not surprised. Really, I think he was delighted, first of all to get rid of us and second, anybody on the road in those days was a paper hero, and we had become Mark's good friends.

We headed toward the Gulf on a little jungle highway as dark as pitch. There wasn't a car anywhere that time of night so we turned off the headlights and skimmed along by the light of the stars. The atmosphere was close and steamy, and myriads of electrified locusts buzzed and whirred through the countryside as we made our way along in the darkness. It was so hot even with the windows down that we couldn't stand it, and I finally decided to try riding up on the roof to catch the wind. It worked pretty well. So I would take a turn and then Mickey would take a turn. Thus it went, out through Trenton and north up Highway 98. Along about four a.m. we got sleepy and turned off the road to spend the morning in slumber.

Later that morning, when we were on the move again, Mickey said he thought the van was too shot to make the trip clear out west. I didn't know a thing about engines, and when he said he was afraid it would blow up, I got a picture of a hydrogen bomb going off right there between us.

"Man," I said, "what are we going to do?"

"Why don't we trade it in on something else?" he suggested.

"Well," I said, "I don't care. I mean, it's your van. Whatever you want is all right with me." That was a big business deal as far as I was concerned, this far away from home, but it didn't seem to bother Mickey. "How do you know it's going to blow up?" I said, not a little apprehensive.

"I can tell by the way it sounds," he said. "I don't know, it may not. I just have a feeling somehow."

"Well, let's get rid of it before it goes." I could just see myself flying out through the bush with sprockets and springs and hot bolts all over the place.

We were trying to get to Pensacola by the afternoon to look through the car lots when we picked up a couple of hitchhikers. They were Jim and Tom, brothers, from Pennsylvania. Strangely enough, they were also in the market for a car. They had driven someone else's car to Florida and made enough money doing it to buy something for themselves. So when we hit Pensacola, it was car lot after car lot. Jim and Tom found a little Triumph two-seater and followed us down the row. We finally hit on a car lot that had a mail truck which had been converted into a camper that Mickey liked. The deal was struck, and off we went with Jim and Tom behind us and a hundred dollars to boot. That night we took a shower in their motel room just outside Mobile, Alabama, and hit the road into the dark.

We rolled across into Mississippi around midnight and started looking for a place to sleep. Thinking we'd just get off the highway and head into the thickets, we were surprised to find that there were little houses and shacks everywhere down through the steamy bush. This dirt road and then that always revealed more shacks and barking dogs. Finally we got out into a wild section and turned into a thick wood to sleep.

This was our first night in the "SO3" and we were really going to enjoy ourselves in our new quarters. We opened all the doors and windows and laid out on top of our sleeping bags.

111

Mickey was up on the wide picture-window dashboard, and I was on the floor between the two padded benches in the rear.

That was my first and last stay in Mississippi. Mosquitoes as big as bumble bees joined us for the night, and we thought we would be stung to death. Swat and fan and bury our heads under hot pillows, sleep was out of the question. After about twenty minutes of battle, we decided we'd have to get out of there and get the beasts out of the cabin before we would ever be able to sleep at all. Mickey headed down dirt roads and pothole lanes with me lying on the floor fanning our friends out the back door. Finally we found the paved road and off we went with all windows and the big back door open. The wind was whipping the little devils past me in the moonlight. Soon the van was cleared and we started closing ourselves in and looking for another place to stop. It was a dark exit where we got off. Mickey drove in a short distance and decided it was as good a place as any. The rest of the night we sweltered in the closed-up camper, but it was better than being eaten alive. My arm had swellings like eggs in a couple of places, and wherever the flesh had been exposed there was a covering of painful welts.

In the morning, Mickey woke me with, "Hey! Look at this!" He was sitting up on the dash. "We wondered where we were last night?"

Out the bay windows I saw a huge lawn with little posts and sidewalks across it. "What is it?" I asked.

"Look over there," he pointed. Back across the lawn was a building with windows across the rear looking out on the field. I still didn't know where we were. "It's a skeet-shooting range," Mickey laughed. We had driven right across the parking lot and up onto the range itself. There we sat, level with the shooting positions. It was only seven-thirty in the morning, so with no one about, we slipped through the gate and up to the road.

Later that morning, we met Jim and Tom on the Gulfport Beach and headed into New Orleans. When lunch-time came, some locals showed us to a little bar in the black section where we got a huge platter of black-eyed peas and rice with French bread for only thirty cents.

We left the bar and started across the street when a guy walking the other way looked right at me and said disgustedly,

"You're not a hippie."

I stopped in the intersection with my hands in my pockets. What in the world is this guy's problem.

"What?" I said with a crazy smile.

"You're not a hippie," he declared with a humph. "Your shirt's too clean!" He turned and continued across the street.

When we got to the other side, Mickey was dying laughing. The guy was right, I was not dirty. I bathed every chance I got, even if it was in a creek or pond. The previous night I had showered in the motel and had a clean white tee shirt on. Every society has its standards of appearance whether military, religious or social; I just didn't match up to this guy's standard of hippiness. Mickey was doubled over, "You're not a hippie!" he laughed. "Your SHIRT'S TOO clean!"

We spent that evening in the French Quarter talking to the transients and street people. Freaks were all over the place and friendship was cheap. We met a guy named "Easy" who talked us into testifying in court that evening against the charge that he had assaulted a police officer. We carried a load of people in the SO3 up to the courthouse at dusk. When Easy's case was presented, we filed by, giving aliases and phoney addresses.

Easy paid fifteen dollars and we all rode back to the French Quarter where they had a crash pad on the third floor of an old boarding house. This was the sleaziest den I was ever in. The door opened into a space where an old ratty couch sat without legs right on the floor. The smell was unbelievable — old, rotten, rank, putrid garbage smell — and there it stood — all over the kitchen, and in a heap on the floor next to the moldy refrigerator. The kitchen door opened onto a tarpaper roof which was surrounded by ancient brick buildings. Away from the couch in the other direction were two bedrooms; one was empty except for some trash lying around, and the other had a solitary mattress on the linoleum. The bedroom windows opened onto the street-side of the building and were the only source of fresh air. I spent my time looking out the window. Mickey decided to sleep on the roof outside the kitchen door. I went down to the SO3 to sleep on the street, which was against the law. There was no law that could have made me sleep in that putrid atmosphere. The smell and filth would be impossible to describe; it did, however, give me a bit of understanding about something I had heard earlier in the day, "Your shirt's too clean."

§§§

Our journey took us up through Louisiana, across the corner of Arkansas through the town of Texarkana, then out into East Texas on Highway 82. It was what we called a "yellow road," meaning it was a scenic route according to the map. Rolling down through these lush woodlands let me introduce the character of the SO3.

Right there in the used car lot in Pensacola it had been love at first sight. She was an old Studebaker mail-truck painted blue and white. The driver sat or stood on the right-hand side by the sliding door which could remain open for easy mail delivery. The front windows were slanted out at the bottom making room for the wide dash which was now fitted with cushions like a sofa. The small rear quarters had built-in padded benches on either side which could have supplied a table in the center, had it been there. Various small cabinets and a sink finished out the cabin interior. Then there was the big door in the rear which rolled up into the ceiling like a garage door, leaving the entire back open. While in New Orleans and then while traveling through Louisiana and Texas, we dressed it up with an Eastern Tapestry over the big dashboard sofa and a long macramé belt hanging across the top of the picture window, which we dangled with bells, sea shells and other treasured trinkets.

The little square vehicle was tall and top-heavy and always leaned hard to the outside of a curve. Even going straight down the road, it would rock back and forth, lightly swinging the decorations in a kind of dance that seemed to match the crazy music we blasted over the stereo system. On the sun visor in front of the driver was a large mirror which was a boost to the ego as one could watch the wind whipping through his hair and also enjoy any fanciful costume he might be wearing at the time.

We chose the yellow roads for two reasons. First, we didn't care much where we were going or when we might get there, and we wanted to see all there was to see in-between. Second, the SO3 would only go fifty-two miles an hour at top speed on flat ground. It was just a lot nicer and easier to follow the yellow roads.

It was about noon. Highway 82 was a lazy two-lane road across East Texas through deep green forests and wild April flowers. We were coming out of a stretch of woods. Mickey was driving and I was sitting on the front dash soaking in the scenery. There was a pickup coming toward us across a low meadow when we realized that the trailer he was pulling had come loose and was easing into our lane. My throat tightened and an ache went through my heart. The little wooden wagon was coming straight at us. Mickey was about to head off into the grass — but who knew where the thing might go next? The pickup was coming up the other side of the road, so that was not an option. Just before Mickey swerved for the right shoulder, the trailer moved smoothly back in behind the pickup and off the other side of the road. I watched out the side window as it flew up through the air into the woods and broke into a thousand pieces against the trees.

That night we camped by a little lake where we washed and shaved with our mirror standing in a dead tree. After we ate and were sitting at the fire, we noticed a strange phenomenon at the end of the lake. Against the blackness of the underbrush was a dazzling display of little whirling lights. We thought it was from the heat or the moonlight, but could not be satisfied until we walked down the shore in the dark to investigate.

"Fireflies!" Mickey roared. "Man, did you ever see such a sight?" I had never seen one in my life and Mickey had only seen a few. This was beyond our imagination, thousands of them circling, diving, sailing, and twinkling in the tall grass.

We caught a few with our hands and then Mickey had an idea, "Hey, they say if you put them in a jar, they make a lantern."

We found a nearly empty peanut butter jar and I went down to the water to wash it out. It was like thick axle grease in the cold water, but with the help of the sand, I came up with a pretty clean container. The next thirty minutes found us chasing all over the woods for lightning bugs, and it was well worth our effort. We hung the jar in the top of the camper and enjoyed nature's luminaries for an hour or so.

Mickey was wanting to go to sleep, but I was all zinged up, so I took a stroll down the lake. Never once did I find solitude when I didn't find that unsatisfied thirst for the divine hammering at my heart. I could wash like a cowboy in a Texas lake and chase bugs like a child around its shores; I could see the most beautiful scenery in all the world and look through the heavens above; but the eye is not satisfied with seeing nor the ear filled with hearing. Frogs were croaking, fireflies were mating, spring was throbbing. Oh, how my heart did long to know God, to be with Him like a friend. There was His new moon, His forest and His lake, even His little fireflies, and I so very lost, yet conscious of it all.

We journeyed toward Denver up across the high edge of the plains. The Rockies looked more like heaven the closer we got. After a day and a night in Denver, we drove to Boulder where we did some looking around and washed our clothes in a laundromat. That evening we headed up into the mountains with some guys who were camping in Four-mile Canyon.

Feeling mean and unshaven
Wearing six-guns and boots
Walking into Denver knowing
I hold my own with any man
Feeling mean like a lion
Riding high on the earth
Walking Mother Nature knowing I am alive
I hold my own
Rocky Mountains over Boulder
Wearing thunderheads and rain
Blowing over Colorado thunder and stone
I hold my own with any man.

§§§

Four-mile Canyon out of Boulder
proved to be a mountain stream
with campfire beans
And a very fine hike to at least one peak
Could have stayed here for ever
but I know this is just the beginning
It's sprinkling now
and Four-mile Creek carries mud and
snow toward Denver
This place slowed me down

116

and now I can see each blade of grass
individually
Bits of snow here and there
say that summer will soon run rampant
through these parts.

After a couple of days in the mountains, we started toward
Cheyenne, Wyoming, on Interstate 25. We spotted a red dirt road
leading off to the east into the hills and pine trees. We had no idea
where it might take us, but we were tired of the interstate and off
we went. It turned out to be a great ride over hill and dale for miles
and miles. We simply took every major junction in the maze to the
left, and late that afternoon we ended up hitting Interstate 80.

Our primary destination was Salt Lake City, where my
brother and his family lived, but we were finding it difficult getting
over the great divide. Out between Cheyenne and Rawlins we got
down as low as twelve miles per hour. Poor old SO3 was putting
out everything she had, but we had to drive on the shoulder with
the flashers on most of the way up to the summit.

There were hitchhikers all over the place and we kept a full
load most of the time. One guy got irritated because of our turtle's
pace and demanded to be let out, he was really grouchy and we
were glad to see him go. After dark, one of the riders pulled out a
pistol and started bragging. We got a little tense but tried to act
cool. When we pulled into a gas station just outside of Rawlins he
went next door for a Coke — and when he got back, we were gone
and his stuff was lying by the pumps.

That night we slept in a desert-like area and the next day
made our last shot up to the Continental Divide. We were crippling
along the shoulder with a capacity load of hitchhikers and were
scared we might meet the guy with the gun; but as it turned out, the
only one we passed that we knew was the guy who had been in
such a hurry the day before. There he sat on the roadside not far
from the summit with a scowl on his face as we crawled past.
"Slow but sure" was our motto and, sure enough, Salt Lake City
lay right on the Utah flatlands when we rolled out of the
mountains.

Al, my brother, was a branch manager in Salt Lake City for
a large national coffee company. His business was mainly with

restaurants, and in the Mormon capital of the world, he was doing a land-office business. We spent a few days with his family, and then had to climb one more mountain before leaving the Rockies. We put in a good hike to the head of Stairs Gulch where we spent the night in the falling snow. Then after another couple of days with Al, we started south through Provo and on toward northern Arizona.

Somewhere down in that wide, green valley south of Nephi, we made a plan for a little fun with the next hitchhiker. And there he was now, sitting on a bridge railing wearing a Teddy Roosevelt hat with the front brim pinned to the peak, a perfect prospect for our game. Mickey was driving, and when he pulled up to where the guy was standing, he just stopped the truck, climbed over onto the dashboard sofa and said, "Hi, you're driving."

"You want me to drive?" he said as he looked in the door.

"Yep," Mickey returned. "If you want a ride, you're driving."

"OK," replied the stranger, handing Mickey his pack.

He greeted me and then he said with a big grin, "All right! Where's the gas pedal on this thing?" He knew we were teasing him and he played into it quite good naturedly.

"Right there," Mickey pointed. "And if you want to drive standing up you can use that one down there."

He put it in drive and off we went. It was no simple thing to drive standing on the right-hand side of the vehicle; the tendency is to position your body toward the center of the roadway. It's a real battle with the senses for the first few miles, and only now had Mickey and I gotten to where we could do it without conscious effort. We all had a good laugh, and before the sun ever set, we were fast friends with Fred.

The conversation finally turned to the subject of the Deity, the existence of God. Fred was a professed agnostic and doubted that there was a God but couldn't be sure. Mickey and I were both strong in our beliefs, his dad being an old-fashioned preacher and I being an admitted seeker of the Absolute Reality which I was sure existed in the Supreme Being. The discussion went on and on as we drove down through the dark pine forests of southern Utah and eating Fred's raw asparagus.

The miles were piling up behind us, but the solution to

118

Fred's confusion could not be found. "If there is a God, like you guys say there is," he argued, "then why doesn't He come down here in His sneakers and stand behind the podium and tell us about Himself." Had Mickey and I been acquainted with the truth we were trying to defend, we could have told Fred that God had done just that.

As we came down into Arizona in the wee hours of the morning, the gas gauge was getting closer and closer to empty. Finally we passed a service station sitting in the moonlight, as lonesome as the butte which stood behind it on the desert floor. We pulled off the road a quarter of a mile farther, figuring on filling up in the morning when they opened.

Three people could barely sleep in the van, so I volunteered to bed down outside. I walked up toward the cliff, a good stone's throw from the SO3 and rolled out my sleeping bag by a large stone.

The night sky of northern Arizona is beyond the imagination of one who has never seen it — deep, clear, and crisp. With the nearly full moon, the night was so bright I could see every feature on the face of the plain before me. There was something eternal about it. This was the desert God had dropped me into twenty-four years earlier on the first day I ever seen sunlight. The smells and sounds of the desert never leave the being of one who has lived and grown up there. I lay wide awake for a long time enjoying myself until finally a chilly breeze began to blow and I tucked my head in for the night.

It was the crow of a rooster that awoke me. I fully expected the sun to be breaking over the horizon when I reached my arm out into the cold and flung my cover down to the zipper. I did not realize that roosters have some special sense of timing, and long before the stars ever start to fade, they usually begin their morning ballad. The cool desert air felt refreshing to my exposed face, so with the covers tucked tightly around my chin, I dozed and daydreamed into the dawn. The air was as still as the stars. The crickets had grown tired of chirping and all was silent. The moon had gone down over the cliff and the Milky Way now spangled the deep black sky. Then I was asleep again.

Ah, this was a sweet life, turning with the earth, night to day and then back again as easily. Homelessness had become my refuge and solitude my security. There is a peacefulness that goes along with loneliness, and there is a God in heaven Who is looking down upon the children of men to see if there be any that seek Him. Mickey was running from Him, and Fred doubted His existence. But down in my sleeping bag there lay a vessel that echoed with emptiness, hollow for the filling.

Again the Arizona desert rang with the call of the rooster.

Gripping an ancient split-rail less than a mile away, the great copper bird stretched eastward to claim the dawn that was about to break upon the new day. When I opened my eyes, the sky was beginning to blue; a few stars yet twinkled, but day was well on the way. As the fires over the eastern horizon gathered strength, little wisps and breezes began to play about my cheeks. Finally golden spokes of sunshine reached across the sky above me and the rooster seemed to freeze in the intensity of his cry. I could imagine sparks squeezing from the corners of his eyes. The sun broke over the distant peaks and all my senses peaked with the ringing, spinning, dancing dawn. The bleak red desert was in an experience as total as creation. Like a festival, there was light and color and warmth. My heart was the bass drum and the desert was the symphony. Emotion rose up that almost brought tears. I thought it was the sunrise that reminded me of tears, but actually it was the drum, the beat of my hungry heart.

By the time I had my boots tied, the sun was standing like a shield above the end of the valley. No life yet stirred in the mail truck, so I left my gear and headed up into the hills. As I climbed the ocher ridge, I could feel the desert in my soul. This was Eden to me.

High up on a sandstone boulder I stood looking out over that primitive red valley as one might stand and stare at Plymouth Rock lost in a Pilgrim's dream. Sunlight stood like fire on my cheek and forehead. I had known almost every climate from the Southern Gulf to the Alpine summits, but this one was mine. My senses had been weaned on mesquite and pepper trees. I had been friends with the horned toads and scared to death of the scorpions. I had always loved the smell of desert spices.

When I walked out of the boulders, Mickey was standing in the shade of the SO3 eating an orange. Fred stepped out looking like Ulysses S. Grant with his old boots, army jacket, square beard, and that washed-out burgundy felt hat pinned up at the front with an archaic military medal.

When we pulled out of the gas station a few minutes later, Mickey was driving with Fred's hat on, and was bargaining for it like a Tijuana basket merchant. "I'll give you this truck and everything in it including Brad's guitar if you'll let me have it."

"Man, are you crazy?" Fred laughed. "Why, with the market going like it is, in three days I'll be able to trade it for the Grand Canyon!"

We spent some time scratching through a deserted Navajo hogan north of Flagstaff, but only came up with a rusty bull ring, and an old medicine bottle full of dried mud. By the time we were heading down into Oak Creek Canyon, Mickey was hard at it again for the hat. "Look, I'll give you this bottle of dried Indian mud," he cackled as he watched himself in the visor mirror, "and this rusty ring of White Buffalo's bridle."

Fred grinned and shook his head.

"Man!" said Mickey. "This is quality rust. Just look at that texture. It's ancient, I tell you, ancient."

By the time we got to the bottom of Oak Creek Canyon using the steep, winding road, we had a good line of traffic stacked up behind us. Mickey pulled over to let them by and we received some pretty rough looks, some of curiosity and some of fear. We all had to laugh as one old lady turned clear around in the back seat and craned her neck, her face all screwed up like she was looking through a needle.

"Poor people," said Fred with a mouthful of raw asparagus. "They think we are the weird ones."

We dropped Fred off on Blackstone Highway that evening just after sunset; he was still wearing the felt hat. As we crossed north Phoenix, the thick fragrance of orange blossoms was almost visible. The towering palm trees and clean hot air were a feast to my memory. And there was Squaw Peak, standing like a rough pyramid against the evening sky.

We spent the night with my grandmother who was a bit disgusted by the way we looked, but she tried hard to conceal it. The chicken and dumplings were all I'd dreamed they'd be and more. In the morning it was biscuits and gravy. Mickey was really lighting into them when Grandma, knowing he was a northerner, asked if he knew what the gravy was made of.

"No, what?" he obliged.

"Just bacon grease and flour and a little milk is all," she smiled and turned into the kitchen.

Mickey leaned over toward me and whispered, "Is it really grease?"

"Pretty good, huh?" I smiled with my mouth full.

Mickey looked at his plate and turned a pale off-white. Not one more bite could he take.

Late that night we rolled down into Los Angeles. The atmosphere was almost demonic, and the closer we got to the center of the chaos, the more threatening and ugly it all seemed. I tried to look up an old friend but had no luck. So we drove well into the morning trying to get out of the city and on our way to Bakersfield.

Chapter Eleven

PRECIOUS CARGO AND GYPSY JUNK

Arizona may have been the place of my birth, but California held the greater part of my memories. The stay with my parents was a welcome rest from the road, and I ran almost constantly on happy memories and familiar atmosphere. I'm sure Mickey and I were an embarrassment to Mom and Dad, but then all the neighbors' kids were turning out about the same or worse. We ate like lumberjacks for two weeks, worked on the SO3, and ended up with at least one adventure worth telling.

The Kern River comes tumbling out of the High Sierras just above Bakersfield, and then meanders through the foothills before it is ordered into a system of irrigation canals for the rich San Joaquin Valley. As a kid I had ridden the rapids many times and was now treating Mickey to a wet, wonderful day. In the middle of the afternoon we came floating by some Mexican kids having a party on the bank.

"Hey!" one of them shouted. "Come on up and have a little wine with us!"

We laid our inner tubes on the sand and joined them; there were three guys and a couple of girls. They had been taking downers and were staggering around on the shore laughing and passing the wine bottle. Mickey and I both turned down the "reds" but helped ourselves to the wine. We were returning their small talk when all of a sudden Mickey's tube exploded in the heat of the sun. "That's no problem," someone slurred. "We'll take you home when we leave." We were almost at the end of our river journey anyway and so we said it would be appreciated.

Mickey and I hadn't had enough wine to amount to anything, but they were really getting smashed, falling all over the place and acting like a bunch of weirdoes. We were kind of wishing for another tube when one of the Mexican guys pulled a pistol and started showing it off. Our eyes bugged out and we began to wonder what we had gotten into.

It was a hot May afternoon and the river was fairly active. Before long three more people came floating around the bend and the guy with the gun shouted an invitation to come have a drink.

They turned him down politely and he started getting irate. "YOU BEDDER GET OU' HERE AN' HABB A DRINK 'R I'LL BLOW Y'R HEADS OFF!!" As they floated slowly away with the current, he went stumbling off through the brush trying to get a shot at them.

Mickey's tube looked like a dead seal-skin lying in the sand. He looked at me like, "What in the world are we going to do?" We were stuck. We had no choice but to act friendly and hope for the best.

We were sitting there faking a wonderful time when around the curve in the dirt road sped a car. All three of our charming hosts started after it on foot, yelling and screaming obscenities. Soon they were back muttering about a guy who had said something to one of the girls earlier in the day. They were wishing they could get their hands on him. We were taking little sips on their wine bottle when the same car came roaring back up the road and slid to a dusty stop. Our three Mexicans walked over to the car and the one with the gun casually stuck it in the guy's chest and pulled the trigger. POP!!

I couldn't believe what I was seeing. My heart strangled me. He tried to get out of the car and fell in the dirt holding his chest. They kicked him up against the rear tire and worried him like a helpless child. Then finally he struggled to his feet, fell back in the car and sped off, leaning half out the door.

I knew I would be next if I didn't keep my cool. Mickey and I both just acted like these were the things we really enjoyed and everything was peachy.

Finally they said they were going to head to Bakersfield and we climbed in the back seat. They varroomed wildly around the dirt roads and off up the little highway. When we got to the top of the bluffs, we had them let us out; we said we didn't have far to go and thought we'd walk across the college campus on the way. As they drove off, leaving us standing on the sidewalk, we both came unglued, shaking all over and talking at the same time.

§§§

Mothers have the peculiar ability to believe their own kids are really pretty good, clean kids. The following week when

124

Mickey and I headed for the ocean, Mom could honestly believe in her mother's heart that we were just out for a healthy time of swimming and sightseeing and would then be home for more of her good cooking. I'm sure she wondered what kept me on the go all the time, and no doubt she wished I would settle down and get married and have a family like other young people my age. But there was something in my blood that only said, "Move on." Satisfaction was always resting on the horizon like the end of the rainbow, and I never could quite get to the pot of gold. What can a mother do but pray, and groan, and keep the home-fires burning with a love that does not give up in the face of heartbreak?

After our trip to the Southern California beaches, we showed up at home for a few more days, and then it was time to hit the road again. Mom saw me off with kisses and sandwiches, a big bag of fruit, and twelve dozen cookies. We waved good-bye and drove straight over to the ocean, hit Pacific Coast Highway in San Luis Obispo and headed north up Big Sur.

It was after dark when I located the canyon where I had stayed with the river commune freaks back in AWOL days. It was too dark to climb up through the rocks and logs, so we spent the night in the SO3. The next morning we hiked up to the camps and looked around, and spent the night among the ferns and redwoods.

Our next major point of contact was to be San Francisco. We drove up past Monterey and Fort Ord, and the scenery brought back memories, fond and otherwise. I related some old war stories to Mickey and a hitchhiker as we continued around the bay toward Santa Cruz.

It was just after noon when we pulled into Santa Cruz. Mickey was buying gas and I was looking around. What a fine town. I took a conscious breath of clean ocean air. Although I had been to Santa Cruz once before, this was the first time I saw it for what it really was; mountains, ocean, giant redwood forests, blue sky, and crisp air. But then I wasn't the first hippie to get infatuated with Santa Cruz; the town had been at the heart of the hippie movement since it began, just as Berkeley had been at the head, and Haight-Ashbury at the foot.

"You know, Mickey," I said as we pulled into the street, "if I ever get through traveling I think I'll settle in Santa Cruz."

"Really?" he answered, "Why Santa Cruz?"

"It has everything, mountains, ocean, trees." I was taking it all in as we rolled through town. "I don't know, it just seems like the town for me if I had to have a town."

Just up in those mountains, tucked in under the edge of the redwoods, the Walrath farm was the scene of constant activity. The names and faces of the young people were always changing. There were those who had arrived in disgrace and had gone in victory, as it had been with Steven and Sandy Palm who were now attending Bible college in Illinois. Then there were those who had come in from the world and gone back to the world, leaving behind heartbreak and tears. The change that was taking place now, in the summer of 1971, as Mickey and I rolled through Santa Cruz, was a change of pastors for the local church. Reverend Miller was moving to another church, and there was much discussion around the Walrath home as to what should be done about getting a new pastor to fill the position.

By now the group was worshipping in a rented building on Elm Street not far from downtown Santa Cruz. They all felt the necessity of having another man come in quickly as the work was progressing with so many brand new people. Then it suddenly became obvious that the man for the job was living right there under their own roof. It was Steve Hastings, a young man who had been living at the Walrath's since spring. He was already doing some preaching, and the post was offered to him. Steve had come out of the world of mountain beer joints and morning whisky, and his story goes something like this:

Living in the little town of Quincy, California, high in the Sierra mountains, Steve Hastings had operated a little two-pump gas station. He was single, and when he wasn't tinkering with a greasy automobile, he could be found in the bar down the road. One night on his way home, he picked up a hitchhiker, and it seemed all the guy wanted to talk about was Jesus and how he had recently been saved. Steve kept trying to change the subject, but the fellow kept talking about how he had been on drugs and tobacco and alcohol, how miserable he had been, and how Jesus had delivered him. Steve was relieved when the guy got out; he said his name was Robert, and if Steve ever wanted to talk about spiritual things to get in touch with him. As Steve drove away, he was overcome with powerful conviction, and in spiritual misery that he spent a fitful night.

The next morning he went to work feeling very aware of the terrible pain of sin. He had run the station many mornings with a miserable hangover, but this seemed worse than any hangover. The burden was so great that he could hardly operate. When his hired man got there early that afternoon, Steve was gone in a flash, heading for the college, where Robert said he was a student. As he drove up to the buildings Robert was miraculously standing right there. Steve pulled over and casually offered him a ride. Robert accepted and before they ever got to town Steve was asking him if he would come to his house and talk about religion.

When they got to Steve's house, Robert stepped next door for a moment to speak to a friend. In the meantime, Steve hurried in and busily shoved beer cans under the furniture, dumped ash trays over the full garbage can, and stuffed magazines under sofa cushions. When Robert came in, Steve said he wanted to hear more about this "being saved" business. Robert, young and zealous and void of tact flatly declared, "You need to pray."

"Pray what?" Steve asked.

Robert read him a tract on the subject of salvation and had him repeat the sinner's prayer which was printed at the end.

"Lord, have mercy on me, a sinner," Steve repeated with his whole heart, and right there the assurance of sins forgiven flooded his soul. All the painful misery was gone. In that moment the peace and joy of Jesus Christ became a wonderful reality in his heart.

Steve's gas station business was on the rocks. He and Robert attended church and spent a lot of time together. Steve grew quickly in the things of God, but finally his business hit the bottom and he had no recourse but to sell out.

That spring, 1971, Steve went down to Sacramento. He was living in his car and trying to find work. He had only been there a few days when he heard on the radio about a revival in the city. He decided to attend. At the service that night he was introduced to the Bible Missionary Church and Evangelist L. S. Boardman. Steve attended every night and was getting so much help for his newly converted soul that when the meeting was over Rev. Boardman, knowing Steve's need of a home and a job, invited him to accompany him to Santa Cruz where he was to hold another revival meeting the following week. Steve was more than happy to follow the evangelist.

Once in Santa Cruz, Steve Hastings met the Walraths and was taken into their household immediately. By the time the revival meeting was over and Rev. Boardman moved on to his next meeting, Steve had become one of the happy residents of the "Glory Hill Farm."

Now, the middle of summer, he was not only a resident, but he was the new pastor. Yes, the Walrath farm was the scene of constant change and activity.

§§§

Mickey surprised me on the way to San Francisco with a secret he had been keeping. He had called home and talked with his boss who had promised that if he got back to Toronto by the first of July, he could have his old job back. I went cold with the news. I had plans for a long summer, and maybe even a winter on the Baja Peninsula. I could see now that we wouldn't even be able to stop in San Francisco. Oh well, the whole wide world was right there to inspect anytime I took the notion. So, with changing horizons, I reconciled myself to a quick trip back to Toronto. Who knows what would turn up next.

Going through northern California we picked up a guy thumbing his way to Washington State. "Where you headed?" he asked as he climbed in and laid a roll of blankets on the floor.

"British Columbia," Mickey answered with a hint of drifter's pride.

He said his name was Bill. His blond dirty hair hung straight down from his sweat-stained cowboy hat. I noticed he had a knife belted to one hip and a small leather pouch hanging from the other that looked like it had been seasoned on a service station floor. He said he was heading to a "rock festival" somewhere up in Washington. As he commenced to tell of every rock festival he had ever been to, including Woodstock, I leaned back against the side window and moaned silently. He bragged on about how "Country Joe" had invited him to play the guitar with him in New Port just that spring. He told us one great attribute of himself after another until Mickey asked him if he wanted to drive. That at least changed the subject for a while and in the silence, we shared peanut butter sandwiches and apples.

At the Oregon border, we picked up a couple of girls going to Seattle, and before they got settled in good, we took on a guy from Boston who was on his way to Alaska. The little cabin was so full of people and sleeping bags and back packs that we were all laughing trying to find places to sit. Mickey was driving, and Cliff, the guy from Boston, was sitting on the floor by his expensive camping equipment. I had crawled up on the huge mound of luggage in the rear. Bill was sitting cross-legged in the picture window telling one of the girls what a great guy he was. We went that way for miles, listening to Bill and rolling our eyes at each other. My old guitar was sitting around somewhere and the other girl, who had been trying to read, challenged Bill to play a tune since he had been playing with "Country Joe and the Fish" just that spring. He was given the instrument before he could get out of it, and he started plunking around like a ten-thumbed caveman, tuning and retuning, plunking and replunking. Finally he said it was such a cheap guitar that he just couldn't do a thing with it. That it was cheap was no secret, but with unstated satisfaction, we all rested the case.

About midnight, we stopped at a rest area somewhere in the middle of Oregon where we guys slept under the stars and the two girls shared the camper. The next day we dropped the girls off in Seattle and were happy to find that Bill had decided to follow them. I don't think they were too thrilled with the idea, but Bill was the kind of guy that didn't know a hint from a sledge hammer.

We started for the Canadian border with Cliff and his big orange backpack. Some fifty miles up the highway we spotted a van with Alaskan license plates and started flashing our lights until he got the message and pulled over. We introduced Cliff and begged him a ride, which was quickly granted.

That afternoon Mickey and I crossed the Canadian border and pulled up to the customs booth. "What are your citizenships?"

We answered, and then the officer asked Mickey if he had purchased anything while in the States . "This truck," he complied.

"Take this," the man handed Mickey a pink slip of paper. "Park right over there and another officer will assist you."

We parked by the grey building and a girl in uniform led us

through the heavy glass doors. The man at the counter asked to see the van and we all walked out together. I sat on the padded bench in the rear and the officer sat on my old flying from of college days which had replaced the tapestry on the front dash. Mickey stood at the steering wheel and we waited silently. The customs man looked the cabin over with steely eyes. His uniform, hat, and badges were quite a contrast to the interior of the SO3 which was by now a hilarious conglomeration of precious cargo and Gypsy junk.

"All right," the officer eased into a grin, "where do you guys keep the dope?"

We all had a big jittery laugh, and then he gave us the news: Mickey, being a Canadian citizen, could not legally enter Canada with a vehicle purchased in the States in the last six months without paying a stiff tariff. We were already wondering where we were going to get money enough to make it all the way to Ontario, paying customs was out of the question.

We headed back across the border dejected. When we got to the booth at American customs the man heard our story and gave us a pink slip of paper and told us to go in the grey building where we could talk to an officer. The man at the counter took the paper and stepped into an office. Finally he returned looking a bit bewildered. "The United States may not want you guys either," he grinned.

Mickey looked at me like he could kill somebody, "Well! I guess we could just camp out here on the grass, but I don't know where we'd go for groceries!" He said it looking at me but the customs officer got the message. He said he would be back in a minute. It was a long minute, but he finally came out and told us we could go back into Washington.

"Man!" Mickey roared when we got outside, "You'd think we were trying to hijack the Queen or something!"

§§§

Our trip across the northern United States on little jointed highways was fairly uneventful. The Rockies were beautiful but we had no time to tarry as the first of July was just days away. We spent one night with "Montana" at his parents' home east of Great

Falls, and sold most of our stereo equipment to a friend of his for gas money. Crossing Minnesota we ate our last loaf of bread and the remains of the peanut butter and jelly. By the time we hit Wisconsin we were down to rice and potatoes and some chicken flavoring my brother had given us. I cooked up a horrible stew on a rest area bar-b-q and we filled our stomachs and were off again. We drove all night, through Michigan's Upper Peninsula, and by the time the sun was coming up we were chugging down Interstate 75, wishing for enough gas to get us into Toronto. Mickey was supposed to be at work first thing the next morning and the pressure was on.

I don't know what we thought we were going to do when we got the SO3 to the border again — try to lie I guess. But that was a problem we never had to face. By noon we could see that the gas would never hold out. We had already sold everything that was marketable, and when we pulled into Saginaw we had sixteen cents. The gas gauge was sitting on empty.

"Sixteen cents worth of regular," I said through the sliding side window to the attendant. He looked at me like I was joking. "That's it, man," and I held out two nickels and six pennies.

We went from one car lot to another, but no one wanted to buy a blue and white Studebaker mail truck. Finally on the last gravel lot we sold her for two hundred dollars. An hour later we were on a Greyhound heading through the night for Toronto.

Just two hours before Mickey had to be at work, the bus pulled into the city. He took off on a dead run for the Go-Train, and it wasn't very long before I was walking up the back steps of the apartment I had shared with Bob the winter before.

Was it a hero's welcome, after fearlessly exploring the entire continent from Florida to Seattle and back again? The back door was unlocked, Bob was gone, the first thing I noticed was the smell, then I saw dog droppings all over the floor. The second thing I saw was the empty bird cage on a cluttered table. Jesus Sky Pilot was gone. The third thing I saw was a brand new guitar sitting in a chair. I got it down and gave myself the hero's welcome I deserved.

> I'm a gambler and a drifter
> And I'm not sure where is my home

On a showdown every sundown
And I'm not sure where I am bound
I'm a man now and alone now
And I'm no longer just twenty-four
I'm a hundred, I've climbed mountains
But I never found the key or the door
I'm a thousand, I've heard stories
But they never told the key or the door
I'm a man now, I've seen visions
But I've never seen the key or the door

I walked down Lakeshore with the guitar to visit some friends. The welcome there was a little more what I expected, but before long I was back in the empty apartment waiting for Bob to get home from work. He never came. I finally called his brother.

"Oh," Chuck greeted me, "he's up at Nancy's mom's cottage. Won't be back till Sunday or Monday."

I called Mickey and got the impression his hero's welcome didn't amount to much more than mine did. He came over in his Dad's car and we went down to the Rex restaurant for a Coke. Mickey knew nearly everybody in the area, and as the gang began to trickle in, we became the interesting drifters we felt we deserved to be.

The next evening Mickey and I headed to Georgian Bay and surprised Bob who was playing with his new puppy in the shallow water. Now this was more like it: surprise, questions, friends, admiration. It would have been perfect if Nancy's mother hadn't been there to pose a few questions that we couldn't answer with a nonchalant drifter's poise. In fact she saw through the whole thing and even had the nerve to prove that what we meant by "living off the land" was nothing more than bumming and mooching off established people.

The next day Bob and I were driving out to the store for some pop and stuff when he asked me if I was interested in making another trip around the country. I wondered what he was up to but I didn't have to wait for the rest. "I'm serious," he said. "I'm sick of the rat race. I've got to get out of here for a while. I need a new outlook, or context, or something. This city and job and everything are driving me nuts."

"You really want to take off and leave it all?" I asked, knowing what happened to Mickey about the time I thought we were really getting started good.

"I've been thinking about it a lot," his eyes were still on the road. "I really think it's what I want to do."

Raya the puppy was licking my face happily. I was sort of laughing, but silently I was wondering what the deal was.

"Well?" he looked over.

"Look, I'm ready anytime," I said. "I just need to hear more about what you have in mind."

"I mean I'm ready to go," he was excited just thinking about it. "I'm ready to quit my job this week and get rid of my car and take off."

"Well, man, you're talking to the right guy," I was excited too. "When do we leave?"

"I'll give them my notice at work Tuesday. Then all I've got to do is sell my car."

"How do you want to go?" I asked. "Hitchhike?"

"That's what I thought — that OK with you?"

"All the better," I said. "That would be my choice anyway."

It almost killed me to wait thirty days, but somehow I survived. When Bob's rent ran out in the apartment, he moved in with his parents, and I moved to the woods just a mile from their home. I had been welcome in their house before, but I guess by now I was getting to be a pretty freaky character and they didn't even want me around the place. Bob kept me in groceries and let me in his house for a shower when no one was home.

I enjoyed staying in the woods, all except the time my camp was ransacked. After being away for most of the day, I was shocked to find my clothes thrown all around, and my poetry book ripped apart and strewn through the brush. My sleeping bag was sticky with sugar and water and instant coffee. Garbage lay strewn all over the place. It was a real mess. I was heartsick. After I had gathered all my poetry, and found nothing of my clothes and toiletries missing, I felt better. Now all I had to do was clean everything up. By nightfall I was back from the laundromat, all snug and doing my best to forgive the kids who had probably come upon the camp while playing and had done what comes naturally.

For ten days I read books, wrote songs, and played Bob's old guitar (the new one had been borrowed). At night I listened to the groundhogs battling in the meadow and tried to resist the fears that always come to one who is alone in the woods at night.

It was a struggle with patience. I was dying to be on the road again.

Chapter Twelve

REACHING FOR JESUS

Bob's brother drove us to Buffalo, New York, around the first of August, where we set out on foot for parts unknown. We hitchhiked directly south through Pennsylvania, hooked onto Highway 220 and headed into the Appalachians. Hardwood forests, verdant pastures, and little one-street towns were the run of the mill. Mountain boys in hot rods squealing out through the curves, corner groceries with ancient wood floors, bridges over canyon streams in the middle of nowhere — on and on went the wonders of the hills. Throwing the Frisbee back and forth as we meandered through shady woodlands and making long treks across sunny mountain meadows, was the normal turn of events.

One night after sitting at the south end of a little town watching the locals turn around and head back to the hamburger joint again and again, we realized we were out of rides. We laid our sleeping bags behind a billboard and were soon fast asleep. I was the first to be awakened in the early morning by rain on my face. So it was up-in-a-hurry and head for shelter. But before nine we were high and dry in a mud-caked pickup wandering through the most beautiful country east of the Mississippi. By noon the sky had cleared and we were shooting the Frisbee back and forth across a wide turn on the lower edge of a meadow in the Shenandoah Mountains.

We had been in the mountains four or five days when one morning we got in with a guy who said he was heading over to Interstate 81 to do some traveling, if we wanted to go along we could be in North Carolina by night. We went with him as far as he was going and had supper at his aunt's house and took a shower. We could have spent the night there, but decided to try to make a few miles before we got tired. As the night got darker, we ended up on a road that was too big to hitchhike and spent many hours watching headlights speed by.

About midnight it started sprinkling and we began to look for cover as the atmosphere was low and rain was sure. We spotted a big hay shed across a field and out through the mud we went. It was as dark as a night storm can make it and by the time we got to the shed the rain was really coming down. The shed was simply a high galvanized roof supported by steel poles under which stood a gigantic mound of hay. Dry hay, what a spot! We were not yet soaked through, and as the rain rattled on the roof we prepared for a comfortable night in the straw.

Our sleeping bags were rolled out on the comfortable straw, and Bob was about to turn out the flashlight, when I noticed a tick crawling on my arm. A quick investigation revealed a regular army of wood ticks marching onto our bed rolls and into our clothing. We fought, we flung, we picked and scraped, all the time trying to get dressed and packed and out of there. By the time we were running out into the mud and rain, our flesh was crawling with the thought of ticks, Ticks, TICKS! Every rain drop that ran down the back of my neck felt like a tick. Every itch on my leg was pinched and rubbed and squeezed just in case. The open highway was our only refuge, and that was too big and too hostile to get a ride. But where else were we to go except out there to stand in the rain and stick our wet thumbs up into the oncoming headlights.

I guess it must have been pity that caused one guy to pull over. With much thanks we climbed into his dry car. We wanted to get over to Highway 21 which was smaller and we figured easier to get rides on; so after an hour or so he let us off at a little country road that he said would take us to the highway we wanted. The rain had quit, and we sat down to rest and have a smoke before we started walking.

It was against my philosophy as a hitchhiker to walk up the road backwards holding my thumb up as I went. After all, the guy who eventually picked you up would have picked you up two miles earlier. It was all the same to him. And then, if you found a good place, well-lighted where you could be easily seen, a place where a car could get off and stop, I couldn't see trudging away just for the sake of appearances. It was always a good rule to find a good place with all the elements necessary for the convenience of the driver and then make yourself comfortable for the duration.

Bob and I were walking on this particular night because we were now on a deserted little back road which was supposed to take us through the woods a mile or so, out passed some houses, and finally to the road we wanted. We were wet and weary, but we needed to be on the right road first thing in the morning

By the time we got through the woods, my pack straps were rubbing me raw and I thought I was going to die under the load. My feet were blistering in my damp boots and my heavy pants were about to slip off. Bob was in the same shape and we were starting to wonder if the wet was from the previous rain or from the steam that was now cooking us in the Carolina heat. Finally, after a two-hour hike, we were coming into civilization. It was about four in the morning and we were hoping we had our directions right. We knew one thing, his "mile" was more like three or four. By the time we got to Highway 21, we were ready to drop from exhaustion and were more asleep than awake. I laid flat out on the wet grass in front of a commercial building and went soundly to sleep, while Bob tried to keep an eye out for cars.

The sun came up while I was sleeping. Along about eight o'clock Bob shook me awake; a guy had stopped on his way to work. I was lying in the wet grass, and the Southern sunshine had literally baked me. I barely knew where I was or what I was doing as I staggered to the open car and fell in behind the front seat. It was a foreign job and I was crumpled into the back like a rag doll with both back packs. I tried to go back to sleep, but was so physically sick from heat and wet and exhaustion that all I could do was swim in the head. The sun through the windows was like a hot house against my damp clothes.

"Hard times is good times," we used to say. But adventure and romance is adventure and romance when you are reading it. When you are doing it, it's a battle.

Why did we do it? What caused us to get out there and torture ourselves? Well, we grew up in a day when we had everything handed to us; maybe some didn't, but I did. Not that we were rich, not at all, we just had everything necessary to make life comfortable and convenient. Survival was something so foreign that we only heard about it through the media, and it was always somebody on the other side of the globe who was having a rough time surviving. I'm not blaming anyone, we just simply had it made without trying. But there is something down in a man that demands a quest, a challenge, a threat. Call it pioneer fever, call it wanderlust, call it whatever you like. It is something that eats away at you until you say, "I've got to jump up and run out to the horizon and have myself a look. I've got to get so far out on a limb that I can't get back and then I'm going to find out what it means to fight for my very existence. I've got to bite off more than I can chew, and then if I survive, I can look myself in the face."

§§§

When we finally go to Gainesville, Florida, we went right to Mark's house. He was glad to see us. For about two weeks we stayed with him and his roommates, "living off the land", and looking up everybody I had met the first time traveling through with Mickey.

This evening finds him
        making sad music on a friend's guitar
In the pale light of a candle
        he rolls tobacco from a mason jar
He sits and fingers the patches on his jeans
        and recalls a patterned dream

Where went those days
        of snowball fights up in cold Ontario
A silver airplane, a snowman,
        a warm and homey place to go
The candle tells him joy is just a dream
        just a lonely yester dream

And now the life that waits for him
        is burning Mexico
Devils' dens and bloodshed graves
        and midnight's haunting moans
Where everything is scorching,
        crackling mean
        like a nightmare dream

So play that sad old guitar
        and let the tears well up
And sing your songs
        of budding life, raining joy, and springtime love
And wonder why the patches on your jeans,

why the patches on your dreams

§§§

I wish I had a penny for every time
I sat and watched a car go by
I wish I had a nickel for every time
I prayed to Jesus for a ride
I wish I may I wish I might
Have the prayer I pray tonight
I wish for Jesus by my side
And I pray for a ride tomorrow

I wish I had a dime for every time
I slept right down by the side of the road
I wish I had a dollar for every time
It rained on me when I awoke
I wish I may I wish I might
Have the prayer I pray tonight
I wish for sunny days all my life
And I pray for no more sorrow

I wish I had a penny I wish I had a dime
I wish I had a dollar for every time
If I had a hundred just to spend
I'd buy a heaven-ticket, be sure to get in
I wish I may I wish I might
Have the prayer I pray tonight
If heaven costs a dollar bill
I'll probably have to borrow

About the time we felt Mark and his friends were getting tired of supporting us, we hit the road to the Atlantic coast and the little town of Flagler Beach. There we body-surfed and combed the shore and lived by a campfire, enjoying the natural elements.

One night just after sunset, I was sitting working on a song, using Bob's newly purchased twelve-string guitar. The pier was about two hundred yards down the beach and the full silver moon was standing above it. The sky was turning dark on the Atlantic horizon and stars were just beginning to twinkle. Full of faith and hope that God was looking down on me and caring I wrote,

> Tonight I caught the moon smiling down on me
> Smiling down so big and bright and making me feel free
> And I'm crying no more, I'm smiling
> I'm crying no more
>
> Tonight I heard a star calling down to me
> Star whose name is Bethlehem, the Lord is after me
> And I'm running no more, I'm praying
> I'm running no more
>
> I walk on this earth a vessel of my God
> Mountains are my playmates and the sea is my backyard
> But I'm reaching for more, Lord Jesus
> I reach out for You
> Lord Jesus, I reach out for You

Some people who were walking down the beach road heard me singing and stopped to talk. They were interested in where we were from and where we were going. That was the usual small talk. A little later one of the girls asked me why I was living the life of a drifter, what I was after. I remember saying something about trying to find the meaning of life. That must have been a little brief because the look she gave me was still a question.

"Well, let me put it this way," I philosophized. "The moon, the stars, and the sky. The sand," I held out my hand letting it sift through my fingers. "The ocean. The earth we're living on. What's it all about? What's it all here for? And why me? And why you? What are we all doing here?"

There was a pause. I was trying to be serious, but the man in the moon smiled like he had just heard a good one.

The next day around noon Bob was in town and I was straightening up the camp when I heard footsteps behind me. It was the Flagler Beach policeman standing there with his hands on his hips.

"This your stuff?" he asked gruffly.

"Yessir," I said.

140

"Do you know it's against the law to camp in the city limits?"

"I thought we were outside the city limits," I said respectfully. "The sign is just over there across the road."

He didn't answer. He looked around at all of our gear. Then looking back into my face, he pointed his finger at me and said, "You get your junk together and get out of town by one o'clock tomorrow or I'll knock the back of the jail out with you."

"Yessir," I smiled sheepishly.

§§§

After a few more days back in Gainesville, Mark drove Bob and me out to the little town of Suwannee River where we set up for a ride. It took us all morning and into the afternoon to make sixty miles to the town of Perry. In Perry, we got crossed up and had to walk three miles to get to where we wanted to be, on Highway 98, which would take us across the north beaches of the Gulf.

It was a long walk in the frying Florida heat to where we finally settled in some tall grass across from a little trucker's cafe. Car after car sped by as the afternoon dragged on and the heat grew unbearable. It must have been a hundred and five, and we were right out under the tropical sun sweating miserably.

Finally, there came a solitary bread truck, an ancient thing, with a couple of freaks sitting up in the front windows like Mickey and I used to do. They were the first of our kind that had come by in two hours and our spirits rallied. Lying against our packs, we both held our arms up at full length with thumbs out beseechingly. Past us they rolled. The first hope in two hours and there it went. Who knew how long it might be before another load of hippies came by?

We were commenting on the fact that we had been stood up by some of our own kind and were already looking back up the road when we heard a horn sound. It was them! They had come back. When we got in, they were both grinning big. "You guys looked so pathetic lying there in the heat," one of them laughed. "We were going to go on by, but the way your arms went up and followed us together in perfect unison was more than we could

141

stand." They were Chuck and Len, and were going to Kansas.

That night we slept on the white sands of the Gulf shore. The next night we camped by a nice little fishing lake in East Texas, and the third night they let us out on the west side of Oklahoma City.

Since we were too close to town to sleep, we started thumbing under a street light next to a ball-field out on Route 66. A car stopped about fifty yards past us and honked. I grabbed my pack and started running. Farther and farther I ran until I began to think something was fishy. I was just about to reach him when I noticed he was rolling slowly away from me. I kept jogging. My pack felt like a buffalo on my shoulders. I was about to fall down. As I got up to the back of the car, he sped away, sending gravel and dust all over me. When I turned around, Bob was sitting under the light almost two hundred yards away.

We finally got a ride out to where Route 66 meets Interstate 40, about twenty miles out of Bethany. There we slept in a field of alfalfa and first thing the next morning caught a ride with a bunch of hippies going to Albuquerque. I think there were three guys residing in the huge delivery truck and there must have been six or eight hitchhikers counting Bob and me. The only one worth describing was a little guy about twelve or thirteen years old, a thumber, who was wearing a full cape made out of a white sheet. Around his little-boy face hung shoulder-length hair, and from his cherubic mouth dangled a long, wrinkled cigarette, wrinkled because he kept them under the cape in his front jeans pocket. Everything about him looked like the freak's freak, the old man and the sea, the sage himself. But that sweet face made the whole thing comical. Who knows, maybe back home he had a mother who was worried sick about her little run-away boy; or maybe somewhere in a nasty hole there was an alcoholic wretch, cursing and swearing and destroying herself, along with everyone she touched.

West of Albuquerque we slept on the dirt. By noon the next day, we were sitting in the back of yet another van. This one carried us all the way to my folks' door in Bakersfield, California.

§§§

I told my parents I was planning to go up to Santa Cruz and try to get a job and settle down. They were seriously interested in my finishing college and continuing in the field of commercial art. They offered me the deal that if I would enroll in the college in Santa Cruz, they would help me get settled by paying one month's rent, enough to give me time to find work. I didn't have to think about it very long. It sounded good to be going back to school and getting my life into focus. I knew I wanted to live a lot better in the future than I had been the last few years. By now I was genuinely sick of the mess I was making of myself. I was sick of drugs, sick of the road, sick of hippies, sick of everything.

On the way to Santa Cruz, Bob and I spent a week up in the canyons of Big Sur. Our routine was to wake up after a night on the hard ground, wash in an icy stream, cook breakfast over an open fire, and drink fresh mountain coffee through a lazy morning of conversation and guitar. The afternoons in Big Sur were spent hiking and exploring, maybe writing a song, and then finally a slow sunset over the Pacific which lay miles below against the foot of the mountains. But September was coming on and I had to get to the University of Santa Cruz for enrollment.

When we went through Monterey, I showed Bob around Fisherman's Wharf and Cannery Row, and then we hooked a ride with some people who were good enough to take us right up to the campus in Santa Cruz. UCSC is one of the most beautiful college settings in North America. High up on a mountain and tucked under an expansive redwood forest at the top of a wide meadow, it looked more like an exclusive resort than a college. We found the administration offices and I introduced myself for enrollment, presenting all the appropriate transcripts and forms from my previous college days.

"Sorry," was the flat reply, "we're not taking any new seniors this year." I walked out into the afternoon sunshine with a lump in my throat. What was I going to do? I was all ready. For the first time in years I had the urge to get back in touch with the establishment, and now this.

We hitched a ride back into town and learned there was another college in the area that I might be able to get into. We got directions, worked our way through Santa Cruz, and down into Soquel. By the time we got to Cabrillo College, the administration buildings were closed for the day.

A half mile away we found a place to camp on the New Brighton Cliffs where we unrolled our sleeping bags under a manzanita thicket and settled in for the evening. On the beach, two hundred feet below, we found an outside shower where we cleaned up the best we could.

At dusk I was sitting alone under a pine tree looking across the bay. The stillness was majestic as the surf crushed softly against the rocks below. The moon was full standing out above the bay, casting its silver rays across the water and into the waves at the base of the cliffs. Some thirty miles across the bay, the lights of Monterey were beginning to twinkle. I was thinking of the previous full moon which I had watched rise over the Atlantic and climb out above the Flagler Beach pier. Then I thought about the song I had written that night, just twenty-eight nights before, which had become my favorite and most often played. "Reaching for Jesus" was actually a prayer, and I had sung that prayer a score of times in the last month. With the words of that song on my heart, I began to converse with the Deity. I had no doubt He was listening in.

"Lord," I said audibly. "You know what I want. I've been searching and searching and asking and asking. Still I'm nowhere. I know You hear me," I said seriously. "I know You have the answers, and I know You can help me."

In the closing darkness, the moon seemed almost cold in its bright whiteness, standing like a shield in the open sky. I sniffed the handful of pine needles I had been rolling between my palms.

Then I thought, "Maybe I'm so ignorant of the things of God that I'm asking for the wrong things. Maybe what I want, and what I really need, are two different things."

"Lord," I flashed, "You know what I NEED! Dear God! whatever it is that I need, please give that to me." Moonbeams danced in the breakers far below. Somehow I had the feeling I was really getting through. "Whatever it is, Lord! I don't care. Just do whatever You must, to bring me to Yourself.

Chapter Thirteen

UNDESIRABLE CHARACTER

I did not want to go back to a junior college, but I had no recourse. The next morning Bob and I walked back over to Cabrillo College and I enrolled in one class, biology. It was the only course I needed to complete my general education requirements, so I figured I'd get it out of the way and then get into another college the following spring.

That afternoon we were sitting on the beach below the cliffs. I was playing the guitar and singing, when a man sat down nearby to listen. I pulled out my favorite song, "Reaching For Jesus." He was very congenial and asked if I'd sing another. It just so happened that the one I chose had something in it about Jesus and by the time I got through he had tagged us "Jesus Freaks." He said he was from back East and was in Santa Cruz on a business trip. Then he said he was a Christian and was interested in the Jesus Freak movement in California. Well, personally I was not too thrilled with the so-called Jesus Freaks. I had been around a few of them and had seen that there wasn't much to their religion. They smoked like we did, talked like we did and just about lived like we did; I just couldn't see adding the title "Jesus" to that. Anyway, the man took an interest in us and asked what we were planning. I said we were going into Santa Cruz and start looking for a job and a place to live. He asked if we wanted a ride as he was going that way and was about to leave. We took off in his rented car.

On the way into Santa Cruz, he offered to buy our lunch. We pulled into a bar-b-q place where we each got a sandwich, French fries, and a Coke. By now this stranger from "Back East" was getting to know quite a bit about us, including the spiritual side of my search. When we were nearly finished eating, he excused himself for a minute and returned with another set of BBQ's, French fries and Cokes. He said he knew we were still hungry and he wanted to help us out.

When we went out to his car to get our packs, he shook our hands warmly. Then looking me right in the eyes, he told me to keep praying and seeking and I would soon find real satisfaction of soul. As he drove off, I got a chill up my spine and seriously wondered if we hadn't been visited by an angel.

The next day Bob and I started up Highway 9 through Felton, looking for a place to rent with the money my parents had given me. We had no idea how impossible it was to find lodging in that area. It was incredible how we happened on a note in a real estate office which had been left there only minutes before. In fact, when we got to the address, the landlady hadn't even gotten home from town yet.

The house was built on a steep slope and had a big double garage door leading under it. On the outside of the house was a stairway up to the back door. The landlady finally pulled up in a battered old Dodge with a dog in the front seat. She looked quizzically at us as she came up the drive, but then she smiled when she handed her the note she had just posted at the real estate office.

"You guys didn't waste any time, did you?" she chuckled. Then she stuck out her hand, "I'm Doris. Here, help me get these groceries upstairs and I'll show you the place."

There was a porch running along the back of the house shaded by a grapevine trellis. Up the hill was the backyard and garden. After we put the groceries on the kitchen table, she led us back down the steps and opened the garage doors leading under the house. It was a garage basement affair cut right out of the hill. There was a work bench along one side and a utility sink by the doors. A kitchen table sat where the car belonged and the remainder was partitioned off like a workshop and storage areas. Furnished with an old couch and chair and cot, it was a bit rough, but then it was a long way from the fields and mountainsides where we had been sleeping. I took the little pantry with the glass door for my room and Bob laid his sleeping bag way back in the corner behind the "living room."

Now that we had an address, we were eligible for government commodities until we found a job. So the next day we returned with our packs filled to the tops with white flour, bulgur, oatmeal, butter, cheese, canned meat, milk, cornmeal, lard and much more. We even had a whole chicken and some cigarette tobacco.

I started school the next week, and was glad to find I had a ride to Cabrillo with the guy named Tom who was renting one of the bedrooms up in Doris's house. Tom was your average, long-haired college student with a Volkswagen van and a dog named Ark. But Tom was not the most interesting person in the house; that honor belonged to the landlady. Doris was in her forties, hair streaked with grey and a bit of arthritis in her knuckles. She was divorced and lived alone, except for the renters. And she was a freak. At least I always thought of her as a freak; she must have come up in the "Beatnik" generation. She had two sons who were dope pushers all across northern California, and the three of them would sit around casually smoking marijuana together. She fit into the hip scene as naturally as they did.

Doris was just then involved in a big protest sponsored by the local ecologists. The county was planning to put a road right through the natural meadow that lay above the town. The Felton radicals were marching with banners to try to get them to bypass the meadow and reroute the road through the Mount Hermon Christian Conference grounds. The Mount Hermon people were also doing their best to keep the road out of their peaceful atmosphere, and the war was on.

"Run it through Mount Hermon! They're going to ruin our beautiful meadow! Doris was vehement. "Who cares about that bunch of crazy Christians, all they want to do is go up there and pray anyway!" She was really upset, writing letters to the newspaper editors and joining the protest marches at the meadow and at city hall. Her contempt for Christians was no secret, in fact nothing she felt strongly about was a secret very long.

Bob and I were out looking for jobs when we were not at the college, but we soon learned that jobs were nowhere to be found in the Santa Cruz area. I had never had trouble getting a job before; either things had changed or I had changed. I was now a long-haired doper in my mid-twenties, wearing combat boots and wire-framed glasses. The job market for that kind of person was not very wide. I was no longer a clean-cut student looking for summer work; I was a socially undesirable character with a road-worn look. A job didn't exist for me.

One day in our wanderings we came across the city dog pound. We went in to enjoy looking at the animals and I came out with a puppy. I named him Star and he soon became one of us, eating what we ate and sleeping where we slept.

The month of September was disappearing in a blur of job applications, biology lectures, and evenings in our basement-garage with bare light bulbs and cornmeal pancakes. We were quickly coming down to rent time when Doris informed us that the following Saturday would have to be our last day, our rent was up and she wanted us to leave. She said it was hard on her utilities, but I think she was probably tired of my singing in her basement and training my dog to mess out on the lane.

We spent the next day in a fever trying to find another place to rent. We walked down one street and up another all over Santa Cruz but found nothing. And if we had found something, where were we going to get the money for rent? The kindness of my parents was already exhausted. I was sick that evening when we got back to Felton. We had not realized how fortunate we had been to find Doris's place. Now we were about to be out on the streets again with no shelter, no job, no money, and no address to claim for next month's government commodities.

Hey there Mountain Man
They say it's You Who has the answers
They say it's You Who knows what time it really is
Tell me Mountain Man
Just tell me who the truth delivers
They say it's You Who sent the meek to win the world

Just yesterday I nearly made it
But my faith keeps crumbling down
And the truth is right beside it
As my world falls to the ground

What now Mountain Man
If it's true You have the answers
I ask You now why I find dead ends all around
Tell me Mountain Man
Please tell me who the truth delivers
I hear that faith will bring me justice in the end

But don't You know I've nearly lost it
And my soul is tumbling down

And the devil stands beside it
Won't You take me heaven bound

I pray Mountain Man

Can't You feel me reaching toward You
Can't You hear my fading prayer
There's eternity inside You
Won't You give me shelter there

I pray Mountain Man

Tuesday night we were sitting out in the dark talking over our discouragement, positive we'd never find a place by Saturday, and knowing that no hope for a job existed. We knew we were whipped, and the discussion turned to Mexico. I had been planning to go to Mexico all summer and never made it; now it looked like it was our only hope with a cold, wet California winter coming on.

"Ugh," I sighed. "Mexico. I thought I wanted to go, but really, what would we eat, where would we go?"

"I know," said Bob. "Sounded great when we were traveling. Just travel down to Baja, look around, come back." He flicked his cigarette through the darkness across the lane.

We were both trying to imagine what it would be like to survive a winter in Mexico. I'd never been there, but all I could imagine was little grey shacks with full clothes lines, scrawny vegetable gardens, and broken down barrooms with dim lights and rough Mexicans. On top of all that, I could smell the diesel fumes and taste the gravel of the highways. Back on the road again. It made me sick. I was sick of hitchhiking, sick of traveling, sick of weirdoes, and dope and dirt and cold midnights under the stars. I was sick deep down in the middle of my soul.

"Well," said Bob, "maybe tomorrow will look a little brighter."

We walked in and shut the big garage door. Bob disappeared into the other end of the basement. I turned on the light bulb in my little pantry and sat on the edge of the cot. Star jumped up and lay against my leg. I sat with head in hands for a long time. In my mind I could see the trucks speeding by in the night, wind lashing me as I sat by the roadside on my pack. I could see a long deserted beach on the edge of a Mexican desert, a campfire, a dog. I thought of Mexican dope and whisky and vice. Mexican cops and Mexican jails. I thought I could die right there.

Down in my pack, at the bottom, lay my nice black-leather Bible. I took it out and looked at the cover. Mom had had my name inscribed on the lower corner in silver. It flopped open softly and drooped over my hand, brand new. I closed it and shut my eyes. Oh, God, there was a groan that echoed up through my soul like a bad fog. What in the world was I going to do?

Again I opened the Bible, this time to the first page. "In the beginning God created the heaven and the earth. And the earth was without form and void; and darkness was upon the face of the deep. . ." I read down one column of verses and then down the other. I believed what I was reading. I turned the page and finished the chapter, "And God saw everything that he had made, and, behold, it was very good. And the evening and the morning were the sixth day." I closed the Bible and laid it on the pantry shelf opposite my cot.

"Lord," I began. "I don't have a job and I don't have any money, and now I don't even have a place to live." I felt like I had been falling and falling and was about to smash all over the place. "Dear God. . . I don't want to go to Mexico. I don't want to go anyplace. I'm so sick of the road. Lord, I just can't get it together. I can't handle it anymore." Star was asleep at my side, eyelids dancing, feet twitching in the chase. "Lord, I've got to have help. You've got to help me."

I sat in silence for a few moments looking at the floor. The cot was softly rocking with the beating of my heart. Then, in a wonderful sovereign way, the Almighty God leaned down and placed His hands lovingly on the top of my head. A feeling like spiritual honey poured all down through my inner being. Light entered my head and brought heavenly peace into every part of my body and soul. I received a flood of faith and joy that was clearly a gift from above. And then as clearly as He ever spoke to any living man, God said to me, "Brad, all your worries are over. I'll take care of everything from here on."

Star snuggled deep down in the sleeping bag with me and I slept like a baby all night. I had such confidence in God's faithfulness, that it was as easy to trust as to breathe. In the morning I was standing at the open garage doors watching the sun climb over the trees when Bob stumbled out and started washing his face in the utility sink. Star was trotting around in the sunshine smelling the new day as it warmed the rocks and flowers and wooden steps.

"Bob," I said, "we don't have to look for a place today."

"Why?" he looked over his towel.

"We just don't. We don't have to look for a job either," I smiled. "God told me last night He was going to take care of everything. He said our worries were over."

"What do you mean?" he frowned.

"I mean. . . God said He's going to take care of us." I was serious. "He told me last night. He just came right in that pantry and told me."

Bob broke out into a grin. "Really?"

"Really!" I said, "I mean it."

"Well, OK," he said. "What are we going to do?"

"I don't know. Why don't we go down to the river for a while," I suggested. "It doesn't matter, I guess. Anyway, I'm through worrying about it. God said He would take care of us and I believe it."

And that's just what we did. We skipped rocks and explored and watched Star zoom through the brush like a herd of horses. We played and drifted on into the afternoon until we ran out of cigarettes. So we decided to hitchhike to Santa Cruz.

About three o'clock we thanked our ride and started down Pacific Avenue on foot. It was a lazy afternoon stroll, looking in windows and catching the smells of incense and food. The record store was blasting away as usual, and out in front of the St. George Hotel a group of hippies sat in the sunshine.

The Santa Cruz scene was the original handmade wicker basket, stained-glass head shop, hard-rock posters, and potted plants. Barefoot hippies in everything from patched jeans to long robes filled the streets with movement, talk, and music. There was a huge bar and delicatessen called "The Catalyst". It was all open across the front. People, dogs, bicycles and bedrolls cluttered the way through the tables which sat clear out onto the sidewalk. Health foods, bookstores, bakeries and art shops. The heart of the hippie culture throbbed in every window and on every corner.

Bob went into one of the shops and I was continued down the street. As I passed a building with display windows and polished marble walls, I caught sight of myself in the reflection. As I walked along looking at myself, I had this silent conversation -- "You must be out of your head! You haven't done anything all day but play around!"

I felt a little guilty as I looked myself in the face. "You don't have a job! No money, no home, no nothing!" I wanted to look away, but my reflection would not stand for it. "Now you've wasted the whole day skipping rocks!"

I looked myself square in the eye. "That's right," I said, "and last night God told me I didn't have to worry about it anymore." I looked down the street and then back at my reflection. "I believed what God said."

When I got to the corner, I was standing there sort of waiting for Bob when I was tapped on the shoulder. "What do you wear that cross for?" The stranger was referring to the Navajo trinket which had been hanging around my neck on a leather thong for nearly a year now.

I turned around. "I'm a Christian," I answered.

"So am I," he smiled. "Where are you from?" He had on green work-pants, a green work-shirt and black gas-station shoes. His hair was very short and he had a red nose. He was about the squarest guy I had seen in years. I was in no hurry, so when he seemed to want to talk, I sat down on the curbing of a flower bed to listen.

In answer to his questions I told him I was living in Felton and had been on the road all summer. "Where do you live?" I asked, more to keep the conversation going than for anything else.

"I live up above Santa Cruz with some people who are trying to do the will of God," he answered.

Do the will of God! I had never heard those five words put together in that order in my life. A great big bell rang in my breast. "That's what I'm trying to do!" I said.

"Really?" he smiled. "Why don't you come home with me tonight for supper and meet my friends. We have a house in the mountains. If you're interested in doing the will of God, I think you'd enjoy yourself."

152

He said his name was Steve Hastings and that he had been in town doing some laundry and was just now heading home. "You and your friend come and have supper," he said. "We have prayer meeting tonight, so we can bring you back to town when we come."

Before Bob appeared, Steve learned that I played the guitar and asked if I had any songs about Jesus. I told him I had a few. Then he asked me to come to prayer meeting and play them. "We have two guitars at the house," he encouraged. "I'm sure you can use one of them."

Before long, Bob and I were in his dowdy old Pontiac heading into the mountains. I had no idea what I would find when we got to this place he was talking about. I was preparing myself for a communal atmosphere with spacey flower children floating about, some guru types in robes, and at least one old master with a grey beard and sandals cross-legged at the head of the thing.

We drove up a steep hill right through some redwoods and rounded the back of a neat white farmhouse. Steve pulled up at the back door and we got out. He let Bob and me in, and ushered us down a long hall and into a living room with knotty-pine walls and a stone fireplace. Following his lead, I turned into the kitchen where I saw a blond girl sitting at the table with a baby in her arms. "This is Susan," he said. She looked so beautiful I was literally stunned. Her smile was so bright and real. There was a shine on her face.

"And this is Beverly Walrath," he continued, referring to yet another lady who was standing at the stove stirring a big pot of something with a wooden spoon.

"And this is Brad and Bob," he finished.

Beverly smiled with genuine warmth. She was dressed like Mother Hubbard in a long dress with a high collar. She had on old-fashioned shoes and a motherly bun on her head. I thought to myself, this is no guru.

"Hello, boys," she said. "We're sure glad you're here. You'll stay and have supper with us, won't you?"

We kind of stammered shyly. This was unreal. Beverly had that same glow on her face, a kind of super-clear joy. I hadn't been looked at like that since my mother watched me graduate from high school.

Chapter Fourteen

GLORY HILL

A few minutes after Bob and I arrived, a large crowd began to gather around the Glory Hill dining table. We met Keith and Ruth, the married couple who lived in the little cabin just above the farmhouse. There was a boy named Patrick who appeared to be in his late teens, and a young lady named Cyndie with an attractive smile and laughing eyes. Susan sat on our side of the table with her three-year-old son Wesley. On my right hand, at the end of the table, Steve Hastings sat in front of the large cottage windows that looked out across the mountains. Then there was Beverly Walrath, and next to her, at the head, sat Wally, an average middle-aged family man with thinning hair and a wonderfully sweet disposition. They were all the kindest, warmest people I had ever been around.

We ate fried rabbit, mashed potatoes and gravy, a green salad and vegetables. There was cold fresh goat's milk, and for dessert, berry pie. Bob and I ate like it might be our last opportunity for days. What a meal and what interesting people.

After supper Bob and I took a walk around the little farm which was perched on the side of a mountain along the bottom edge of a redwood forest. There was a little pasture below the house and various garden plots of flowers and vegetables. A combined chicken coop and rabbit shed stood up the hill above the grape arbor. Close behind the main house, up on a rocky point, stood the little cabin. A garage and toolshed finished the scene.

Above the upper gardens there was a construction site which they said was to be a barn by the time winter hit. That was where Bob and I were sitting having a cigarette when he said, "You're getting pretty interested in these people, aren't you?"

"Yeah," I admitted. "I've never seen anyone like them."

"Well, I have," Bob took a deep draw on his cigarette and looked out over the miles of redwoods in the great canyon below. "Brad, if you get in with these people, you'll come out crazy."

"What do you mean?"

"I mean . . . I've known people like this. Back in Canada I went to a camp meeting with some of them," he said. "I tell you, they're too far out."

154

I didn't have anything to say, but I did sort of see his point.

"I even went to the altar and tried to pray," he continued. "You'd better be careful. They're just too weird. You'll turn loony if you let them get to you."

Later on we went to church and I was surprised to find that Steve Hastings was the pastor. He was a bit rough, but as sweet as honey. He got up in his work-pants and boots, and a white shirt buttoned right to the collar. It was an informal prayer meeting and we were quickly into the congregational singing. The group numbered somewhere between twenty and twenty-five.

After a couple of hymns, Steve had me sit at the piano bench and sing three of my songs on Patrick's guitar. Then they all got down on their knees and started praying. I had never seen nor heard anything like it. I was kneeling there studying the grain in the pew, listening to them. They prayed loudly for a long time, and after prayer, they each took turns standing and speaking individually. I had never seen anyone stand up at their pew and testify before, and I was really finding it interesting. Beverly stood and thanked the Lord for delivering her from sin some six years before and then proceeded to say that God had kept her above sin, by His grace, down to that good hour; she was glad to be free from sin and in joyful Christian victory. By the time she sat down I was beginning to see Bob's point even more. Living without sin? I knew better than that. I knew a man had to sin every day in thought, word and deed. These people were a bit far out. I felt like getting in the pulpit and telling them how wrong they were; it was really eating on me.

That night after church, Steve took us up to Felton and dropped us off at the end of the lane. All the next day Bob and I combed the area for a job and a place to live, but nothing came of it. That evening we were sitting at the table when a knock came at the garage door. It was Steve. He came in and sat and talked for about an hour and then left.

Friday was our last feverish attempt to find a job and a place to live. We returned to our basement-garage for the last night very discouraged. The cupboard was bare, we were hungry, tomorrow was Saturday, and we were preparing to hit the road south. I heard a car coming up the lane and stepped out to see Steve Hastings' big Pontiac come to a stop. He and Patrick

155

climbed out of the car.

"Hi!" Steve greeted me.

"Hi."

"How's it going?" he asked. "Find a place today?"

"No," I answered. "Nothing."

We were sitting around the table and Pat asked what we were going to do; it was a known fact that we were out of rent and out of money, and without a job. "I guess we're going to start for Mexico tomorrow," I said.

"Really!" said Patrick, intoning his youthful idealism for adventure.

We talked on for a while, and then Steve came right out and asked us if we would like to come up to the Walrath's to live. He said they had talked it over, and prayed about it, and felt that we were sincerely seeking God.

I knew what it would mean to live at Glory Hill. It would mean no smoking, no drinking, no dope, no wickedness of any kind. I also knew that deep in my heart I was so sick of those things, it was refreshing just to imagine living that way.

The next day Steve was there to pick us up. I threw my stuff in his trunk along with a piece of blue plastic drain-pipe of Doris's that had caught my eye as having artistic value. We said good-bye to our landlady and started over the mountain. As we sailed along, I was smoking a hand-rolled cigarette which I knew would be my last. I held it out the window, watched the ashes fly off like sparks and then I let it go. Star was sitting in my lap and new vistas were opening before me.

§§§

Star had been coughing and pussy-eyed. I had taken him to the vet just that week and found he had distemper. They had given me some medicine and said he had a fifty-fifty chance of pulling out of it. By now he was no better and was also beginning to lose weight. I was sad, but kept hoping he would get better. I knew it was highly contagious and that the Walraths had two dogs on the farm; when I presented the problem to them that day, they just told me to pray about it and do whatever I thought necessary. They said their dogs had had shots and probably would not be affected, although it was possible.

I felt it was not right to bring disease to the farm and as much as I hated it, I decided to get rid of Star. He was my little buddy and I had grown to love him, but I knew it was the only ethical thing to do. Steve, Pat, Bob and I climbed up above the barn with a .22 rifle and Star trotted along behind. I was planning to do it myself, but at the last minute I just could not. Patrick volunteered so I handed him the gun. I hugged and kissed Star and walked on up the hill with the shovel.

I was digging when I heard the shot. Tears sprang into my eyes and my lip quivered as I dug steadily on. They came with Star in a plastic garbage bag. It was hard; if they hadn't been there, I would have cried more than I did. I packed the dirt down the best I could and we went back to the house.

there was a dog that ran with me
a puppy
and we were very free
galloping through nature
rivers
grasses sniffing and tumbling
jumping happily
he even smiled at me
we slept together in a sleeping bag
he sneezed on me and we would laugh
and roll over on our backs for more love

I jumped down on the shovel
I heard the shot
I kept digging
I would not cry
Steve brought him up the hill
the hole was deep
I buried him
I pressed his body down
and prayed

The next day was Sunday, and, of course, we all went to church. The crowd was a lot larger than it had been on Wednesday evening. Between Sunday school and the main service, I overheard a hippie girl, who was apparently there for the first time, asking Beverly Walrath if this was a holiness church. Beverly said it was. That was the first time I had ever heard anything about holiness. The girl seemed impressed, although I couldn't tell if it was for good or bad. I listened closely, as I was trying to discover what it was that Bob thought was so dangerous about these folks. I couldn't see anything but kind, loving, clean, happy people. They dressed a little funny all right, but then that was their trip.

Steve preached a clear Gospel message on salvation which was not altogether different from what I expected. That afternoon after a huge dinner, I was out walking alone in the woods when I began to feel positive I wanted to be a Christian, a real Christian, like these holiness people. I made the decision, and then prayed the only prayer I knew to pray; I did what I had always been taught to call "accepting Christ." It was easy. Really, I had accepted Him all along. In fact, I always thought I was a Christian. Oh, well, whatever I had been I now accepted Christ again. Or more. Or something.

When I returned to the house Bob and Steve were sitting on the front porch talking. I greeted them, "Hey, you guys, I just got saved."

Steve looked up smiling, "You did? Good! Where? Up in the woods?"

"Yeah," I said, "just a few minutes ago."

"Well, tell us about it," he said with genuine interest.

"I don't know. Nothing much to tell," I said. "I accepted Christ."

I thought Steve was really happy about it, but now that I know him, I imagine he was a little skeptical. And if he was, he was not missing the truth, because I was no more saved than Bob, who was sitting there growing more angry with the whole thing all the time.

That night in church God really started dealing with me. Steve was preaching a powerful message on the subject of pride and I was getting farther and farther under conviction. I finally tried to tune him out and started running my fingernail along the songbook rack in front of me. The more God revealed my heart, the madder I got. I didn't know a humble hippie had so much pride. I thought worn-out combat boots and patches on my jeans made me unmaterialistic and meek. Steve was not preaching on those things, God was. I began to feel so wicked and vain and proud and worldly that I didn't want to hear another word.

By the time he gave the invitation I was fuming with rage. He was inviting the seekers to the altar. I stepped out to the aisle and strode back to the double doors and out into the night air. I didn't wait for Bob, I went right down the steps, across the street and up to Pacific Avenue.

I walked past a bar with a live band blaring through the open door and a large group of freaks standing around on the sidewalk.

"Spare change," said a tall hippie as I walked past.

I took three steps and stopped, wheeled around, pulled out my wallet and grabbed the only two dollars I had to my name. "Pride!"

"Here!" I slapped the bills into his hand. "Praise the Lord!!" I growled, and walked on, mad.

By the time I got to the end of the block I could hear Bob calling my name. I didn't look back, but slowed down enough for him to catch me.

"What's wrong?" he asked trying to get his breath. "Pride!" I huffed.

"Oh. Don't let it bother you, man. I told you they were off the deep end." He had me where he wanted me. "Look, you don't have to go that far to be a Christian."

"You don't?" I said, not so sure.

"Of course not," he laid his hand on my shoulder encouragingly. "God doesn't expect you to be that weird and straight. Those people have just gone overboard. You'd better stay away from them. I said you'd come out crazy if you started listening to their religion."

I was feeling pretty crazy all right. My mind was flashing around like lightning. It almost felt like the fear and anxiety I used to have in the Army. "Do you think we'd better get out of there pretty quick?" I asked.

"As for me," Bob answered, "I think we ought to go up there tomorrow and get our stuff and leave."

The question was, where were we going to spend the night

with no sleeping bags. It was finally decided that we would hitchhike to Felton and see if Tom's Volkswagen was unlocked. Two hours later found us asleep under the blankets in the back of his van outside Doris Tye's house.

About seven-thirty the next morning Tom got in, started the engine and headed down the lane toward school.

"Good morning!" I shouted.

He almost fell out of his seat, "Wha? . . . Wha? . . . Man! You about scared me to death," he said, trying to get the van going straight down the road again.

We learned he was leaving town that very afternoon for Los Angeles to help his mother move back up to Santa Cruz. He was glad to see us, as we might be willing to help him with her furniture and then drive his van back, while he drove the U-Haul. We accepted, and by the time we got to Cabrillo College, it was all arranged.

Bob and I took the van up to the Walrath's and got our stuff. It wasn't easy. They prayed with us and begged us to stay. They were so loving and sweet, but our minds were already made up and no amount of talking could change us. Something inside me was yearning to stay; but I kept reminding myself what Bob had said, "You'll come out crazy. They're too weird, too straight."

Two nights later we were high up in the Mojave Desert at the house of Tom's friends. They had been growing their own marijuana out on the rocky hills all summer and had a mess of the best dope I had ever smoked. I rolled a fat number all for myself and walked out into the evening for some meditation. Being the desert rat I was, the scenery was highly exciting after living in the woods for so long. The air was clear. It was incredible how far I could see. From where I sat on the southern rim of the valley, I could clearly make out the town of Mojave some forty or fifty miles distant. I recognized the mountain structure around Ridgecrest which was a good eighty miles, and then beyond that I could see the steep edge of the Sierra Nevada's reaching way out past a hundred and twenty-five miles. I was having a thrilling time and I started to do what I had been used to doing for the past four years, I started to talk to God. But something had changed. I tried to think about God and my mind went black. Emotionally I was peaking, stoned on marijuana, in the California desert, under the vast Mojave sky. But a nasty spiritual midnight was strangling my soul and I was confused and irrational.

I got my writing tablet out of the van and sat back among the rocks hoping to bring myself up to a more desirable level. I wrote some of the most pathetic lines in all my material.

God,
I'm holed up on a hill
I'm home without a treasure
without a dream fulfilled
how can I go on living
like this You say it's sinning
I figure if You are out there
God,
hid in the hills
I'll just reach out
and find You

By the time I got to the last few lines my heart was pounding wildly. I literally had to struggle to scribble the last words, "I'll just reach out and find You." Something had changed. A nasty black something was strangling my soul.

I finished the joint, sucking out the last wee drops of poison, then I left the mountainside and went into the house. It was still daylight outside. The evening was young. I lay down on my face in front of the empty fireplace and slept.

My search for God was over.

§§§

Monday evening, the day we had left Santa Cruz, the burden had been on at the Walraths'. Bob and I were prayed for during family devotions. Tuesday morning Steve Hastings had been in the spirit of prayer. God kept us on his heart until he went out to the toolshed to fast and pray. All day and all that night he labored.

Wednesday, as Tom, Bob and I were heading over into Los Angeles, Steve was still at it. Again, all day he fasted and prayed.

That night we were in Tom's van cruising around Los

161

Angeles. I sat in the back and drank warm wine out of the bottle until I couldn't see straight. Before the night was half gone, I had passed out in a drunken stupor, miserable in my despair. All that night Steve Hastings prayed in the Glory Hill toolshed.

Thursday morning we helped Tom load the U-Haul. My head was splitting with a hangover. It was that morning that Steve Hastings walked through the kitchen door with a look of hope and faith on his weary face.

"They're coming back" he said, as though he were dropping dirt on an enemy grave.

Friday, Bob and I drove Tom's van up the coast to San Luis Obispo, with him and his Mom in the U-Haul behind us. After lunch we went up the Salinas Valley and on to Santa Cruz. Saturday and Sunday we helped her get settled into her new apartment.

Sunday evening we hung around the Catalyst discussing our next move. We poked around on our map of California but couldn't find any place we wanted to go. Finally, about nine o'clock, for lack of any other direction, we decided to start toward Mexico and the Baja Peninsula.

As we were walking out to Pacific Coast Highway and our thumbing spot, God started showing me something. I saw clearly, and for the first time, that there was nothing glorified about what I was, or what I was doing. I was not a hero. I was not a rock star. I wasn't even a hippie. I was a bum, a hobo and a vagrant tramp. I was dusty and crusty and smelled like a horse. I was a loser and a zero through and through.

We set up at the corner of P.C.H. and Highway 9 and waited for a ride. It was our plan that we would not take anything that was not going all the way to Los Angeles. We wanted to make it to the Mexican border by the next night. So we turned down ride after ride going only as far as Soquel or Watsonville. We even turned one down to Monterey knowing we were in one of the best hitchhiking spots in northern California.

We were taking turns thumbing. It was dark and we were weary, but we knew our ride would soon sail by and we would be gone, all the way to L. A. in one shot.

It was nearly ten-thirty. A car came around the corner and pulled over. I started to walk back to see how far they were going when I saw Cyndie coming out the front door and Susan out the back with her little boys. Wally Walrath got out the other side and Beverly followed. My heart pounded so strongly I thought I would choke. I couldn't believe what I was seeing. God was all over me. I could have bit my knuckles and run around in circles. Before they got to where I was standing, Steve Hastings' car pulled up behind the Chevy, and he and Patrick and Keith and Ruth started getting out. I was absolutely overwhelmed. I could not get my breath. "These people!" I kept shouting to myself. "These people! It's them! It's them!"

They had had a late night altar service at church, and were on their way home when they recognized us. I stood there like a statue, frozen to the spot. They gathered around us and Beverly asked where we had been. After they found we had been all the way to Los Angeles and back they began to invite us home for the night.

"It's too late to hitchhike now," Beverly said.

"Come home with us and at least spend the night," Steve offered. "Then you can get a good ride in the morning,"

"Where are you headed?" asked Patrick.

"Mexico," Bob said.

I was standing there speechless.

"Oh," Beverly pled, "you don't want to go to Mexico. Please come home with us until you're sure of what you're doing."

"No," Bob said. "We've made up our minds. We're going to Mexico for the winter. Hope to get a ride to L.A. tonight."

I could not speak.

They pled with us to go home with them.

I stood like a wooden Indian, while Bob turned them down again and again. I was yearning and crying in my soul. But Bob was probably right, they were too straight.

As they started to leave, I finally spoke up — "Maybe we'll see you again someday."

Beverly hesitated. "Oh, anytime boys — anytime of the day or night. We want you to know our home is open to you anytime you feel like coming." She was not at all willing to give up, but it looked like there was no use. "Won't you change your minds and come home with us tonight?" They all wanted to talk at once, but what could they say; we had wills of our own and we had decided

163

to go to Mexico. I watched them climb in their cars and head down to the junction of Highway 17 and disappear into the night.

Bob sat down on his pack and I stood up at the side of the road with my thumb out. A wave of sickness swept over me that left me dizzy and trembling. I began to shake like a leaf all over and could hardly get my breath. A great wail came up out of my inner being as the utter emptiness of my life echoed through me. The stars were cold. The trees were black. The road was terrible.

As my trembling grew more intense, I found I was literally shaking in my boots. Then, in that eternal moment, I realized I was standing before Almighty God. The traffic and trees and lights went strangely lucid as the stillness of Judgment seized me.

God put the finger of Omnipotence in my face as He clearly and evenly spoke — "Bradford Henshaw, if you don't go to that house right now, I will never speak to you again." And God was gone.

I was standing on the roadside with my thumb out. The cool night breezes were playing on my cheeks.

"I'm going back," I said loud enough for Bob to hear.

"Huh?"

"I'm going back!" I was still looking into the traffic.

"Back where?"

"Back to that house," I said.

"No, you're not," he said.

"Yeah," I turned to face him, "I have to."

"Man, don't be crazy," he stood up. "We're going to Mexico. Forget those people!"

"I've got to go, Bob. I don't know why. I just have to see what it's all about."

"Well, I'm not going back up there" he said. "I'm going to Mexico."

"Come on," I argued. "Let's just go up and spend the night. We can go to Mexico in a day or two." I was not hitchhiking now, I was defending my soul. "It's not going to hurt us to go up there for a little while. Come on."

"Listen! You can go if you want. I'm not going back with those quacks." He was getting angry. "They've got you under their spell, that's all!"

I stared at the ground. "Look, I'll make you a deal," I said.

164

"If the next car that stops is going south, we'll go to Mexico, if it's going north up Seventeen, we'll go to the Walraths'."

He didn't want to do it, but he finally yielded, "OK, it's a deal."

I was a little scared as I held out my thumb, but I prayed silently, trusting that God was able to stop the right car. It was only a few minutes before a guy pulled over and I asked where he was headed."

"Scott's Valley," he smiled.

Scott's Valley was north; but it was only about half way to Glory Hill. I thanked him for stopping, sent him on his way, and turned to Bob, "Well, that's it. North to the Walrath's."

"Wrong!" he shouted. "I said I'm not going back up there and I meant it!"

"But, the deal…"

"Forget it!" He was mad. "The deal's off. I'm not going."

"Bob," I said. "Look, I'm sorry, but I've got to go up there."

"Well, if that's the way you want it, go then. I'm not."

Bob's pack was larger than mine and had been used to carry both our sleeping bags. Mine was full of my clothes and most of his. We undid everything and separated our stuff on the roadside. The atmosphere was tense and silent. When I got my stuff all situated and was ready to go, I approached the subject one more time.

"Bob," I looked at my friend with whom I had lived, traveled and fellowshipped for almost a year. "You sure you don't want to come?"

"I'm sure," he said.

I told him I wanted to be his friend and that it did not have a thing to do with our relationship, but I was going to go. He said he understood, and we could still be friends.

Like dropping a line in the middle of a school of spawning bluegill, I stuck my thumb into the traffic and hooked a ride clear up the mountain. I got out just across the highway from Glory Hill and started into the redwoods alone. The trees were towered above me in the night, blotting out the moonlight. I was trembling all over. It was like an altar service. I was scared.

"Yea, though I walk through the valley of the shadow of

165

death," I spoke out loud, backpack thrown over my shoulder like a gunny sack, "I will fear no evil, for Thou art with me; Thy rod and Thy staff they comfort me."

I soon broke out from under the trees and could see the farmhouse standing against the forest above me on the mountainside. When I came around the back of the house the dogs started barking and Susan, who was sleeping out under the grape arbor with her two little boys, asked, "Who is it?"

"It's Brad," I answered.

She let out a shout that could have been heard clear to the highway, "Praise the Lord!"

Cyndie was sleeping on the front porch. "What's happening?" she called

"It's Brad," Susan answered. "He's come back."

Cyndie whooped like a train whistle and Susan answered her, their voices echoing against the woods.

I opened the door to the boys' room in the basement and Steve asked who it was. When I identified myself, he welcomed me, and showed me a nice clean bed where I soon laid my head for the night.

§§§

The next morning was Monday. They let me sleep late and when I appeared, they rolled out the red carpet: breakfast and prayer and love and the Word of God. They were concerned about Bob. I told them he had gone to Ben Lomond, a little town up the mountain from Felton, where we knew some people. I think they must have taken the whole day off just to love and bless me. By the time Wally and Keith got home from work the big table was set and I felt like one of the family.

That night they all got their Bibles together and had what they called "family devotions." Wally opened to the next chapter in the succession of their reading and his eyes fell on first Corinthians, chapter eleven, the "hair" chapter. He silently prayed for wisdom; would this truth be good for this new boy who was not even saved yet? The Lord seemed to say that since this was the place they had read to on the previous night, then God could be trusted to keep His economy straight. Off we went through the chapter. Of course, I didn't know a thing about the Bible. First Corinthians, eleven, didn't mean a thing to me. Then we came to, "Doth not even nature itself teach you, that, if a man have long hair, it is a shame unto him?"

The atmosphere was informal. The mood of family devotions was one of openness and frankness and I felt no hesitation in stopping the reading for a question. "Wait a minute," I interrupted. "What's long hair?"

Wally had been expecting it, "Well, Brad. . . now, look at my hair and then look at Beverly's here." Wally had "white-sidewalls" and very little hair at all on his thinning top. Beverly had her long hair done in a modest bun. "Which is long," he asked sweetly, "and which is short?"

"Well, yeah," I said, "I guess I can see that."

Wally was about to read on when I asked, "What about my hair? Is it long or short?"

"Well, it's longer than mine," he started wisely. "Why don't you pray about it, Brad, and see what the Lord thinks about it."

That week at the Glory Hill Farm, I was drawn into the truth and the Person of Jesus Christ through much prayer and Bible reading. For the first time in my life, I talked with holy people, observed their lives, and felt their influence. God faithfully whispered to my heart hour after hour. By the next weekend, I was absolutely confident that I had found what I had been searching for ever since my awakening four years earlier.

Saturday afternoon a preacher named A.G. Johnson arrived. He was an older man with white hair, twinkling eyes, and a heart full of love. Brother Johnson was sitting in the living room on the piano bench that evening telling stories and my heart was melting. His scratchy old voice laughed with every word as his big rough hands joined in the descriptions. I leaned back in order to take in the entire scene. I searched all their enchanting faces. Then my eyes fell on the crackling fire, and for a moment I lost touch with earth itself. For a moment I gazed into a hundred campfires from the Appalachian woodlands to the California coast — I covered fourteen thousand miles of highway, and prayed a thousand prayers — and then I returned to the Walrath's crackling fire, and back into the knotty-pine living room. And I realized I was home.

"Travel light," had said the young man in my dream, "it's not a short walk. Leave behind the things you must."

The next morning was Sunday morning and Brother A. G. Johnson was in the pulpit. He took his text from Isaiah 38:1, "Hezekiah. . . Thus saith the Lord, Set thine house in order; for thou shalt die and not live." He preached about a closet with skeletons hanging in it. His face got redder and redder as he seemed to be pulling my skeletons out and throwing them across the floor in front of the platform. God was dealing with my heart as it had never been dealt with before. Jesus revealed to me the sin that was destroying my life and showed me that I needed deliverance.

Finally, the congregation was standing and all heads were bowed. I was looking at my hands on the back of the pew in front of me. Then I felt a tug, just a gentle nudge at my heart.

"Come on, Brad," Jesus whispered.

I hesitated, not because I didn't want God and truth, but I stood for a moment wondering if this was in fact the final step in my quest for the knowledge of God.

"Is this it, Lord?" I prayed. "Is this really You? The Absolute Truth? The Supreme Being?"

Again that gentle, loving tug, "Yes, son, it's Me. Trust Me now. Come on, I'll go with you."

"Yes, Jesus, I do trust You." I stepped to the altar and knelt down with my nose touching the wooden step that ran around its base. "I don't know what I'm here for, Lord, but I'm here to know You and follow You."

That white-haired preacher knelt over me and began to pray, and it was as though heaven and earth were joined together. It would take the language of the angels who were gathered there to tell it the way it really happened. Brother Johnson told the Lord how wicked and vile I was and how badly I needed salvation. My face was on the floor as I admitted, "Yes, Lord, that's me."

Steve Hastings was behind me and others were praying. Many were seeking at the altar. I lost awareness of everything except the presence of Jesus Christ as I confessed sin, repented and climbed the wonderful ladder of faith. Soon I was crying with an abandon that only God could understand. Then I heard A. G. Johnson saying, "Boy! Don't you think you can believe God?"

168

I didn't know the first thing about what real Christian victory would do for a person, but I did know one thing, I knew I could believe God. "Yes," I answered with my face between my knees.

"Well, son, why don't you just look up and believe Him then?"

When I started to look up, God opened the windows of heaven wide. He poured out a shaft of glory that literally exploded into my breast, and at the same instant I felt sin, like a monster, being torn from the threads of my being. Tears of great relief flowed down my face and my arms sprang up in blessing. God's eternal life was breaking into my soul in wave after wave of liberating grace. I could not have been quiet for anything in the world. I cried for joy. Then I leaped up and turned to see Steve standing a few feet behind me. I started after him on a dead run.

Way in the back of the church, on the old wrought-iron furnace grate in the corner, I caught him. I threw my arms around his shoulders and shouted, "He did it! He did it!" And we rejoiced together in the bond of Christian brotherhood.

I had liberty, I had joy, and I had peace in my heart. I knew I had found the source of all life. I knew I had finally broken through to the great God of the universe and every sin was forgiven. Guilt was erased from my conscience. The blood of Jesus Christ gave me, in an instant, all my soul had ever longed for.

"He did it!" I shouted with unabashed joy. "He did it!!"

§§§

GLORY MOUNTAIN

I found the Lord in California
Up in the country where the mountains meet the sea
When I hit Santa Cruz the Lord was leading me
Out of the darkness into my own destiny
And then like Abraham He gave the plan to me
We all seek someone to belong to
And Jesus is the One we're drawn to

I found the Lord in California
The Son of God revealed the heart of all my dreams
Upon the altar of the mighty King of kings
I laid my sacrifice of empty broken things
God sent the glory of a flaming angel's wings
My spirit came into the kingdom
Now I am one of His own children

Destiny, Eternity
The blood of Jesus sealed my pardon
My spirit stepped into the garden
I could see my Jesus dying
Angels singing and glory flying
on that day
I got saved and I got shouting
On the peak of Glory Mountain
I got saved
Destiny, Eternity

I found the Lord in California
God's holy people prayed a holy prayer for me
They showed me Jesus and they showed me Calvary
I made repentance with my face between my knees
My sins were buried out in God's forgetful sea
The blood of Jesus sealed my pardon
Now I am one of His own children
We all seek someone to belong to
And Jesus is the One we're drawn to

Chapter Fifteen

THE OLD FENCE

There was still a vigorous altar service in progress when I began to realize that the rest of the world still existed. I did not know what to do with such satisfaction and wonder bubbling up in my soul, and so I walked out into the October sunshine to commune with my Savior. I sat on the sidewalk across the street from the church with my back against the block fence. The bright fall sky was a glory of fleecy clouds and the sun was warming me all over. I sat looking at the stout little church with its turret-like belfry; the building lacked any elegance or visual attractiveness, but to me that day it was the most beautiful structure on earth.

I was perfectly aware of the fact that I had just discovered in the realms of truth the existence of uttermost satisfaction. My sick heart had been healed, my lost soul had been found, and my consuming hunger for the knowledge of God had been abundantly filled and was overflowing. Soon the joy was springing up in me until I could sit no longer. I arose and started to take a walk around the block, but before I got past the house next door to the church, I stopped to examine the rustic old fence that enclosed the front yard. It looked like something off the Ancient Mariner; the bulky corner posts were grey and chipped with years of sea air, and the old white paint was chalky and curling off in patches. What were supposed to be the vertical pickets were broken and splintered and leaning. The whole thing spoke of things past. Weeds stood knee-high around the yard. The grass was rank and uncut. The little gate hung precariously from the one old rusty hinge that remained.

I worked a chip of paint off the main gatepost with my finger nail. "Lord," I said softly, "this looks like my life, old and worn and falling down. But I'm going to set the corner posts again and straighten every picket. I'm going to scrape and sand and fix. And then I'm going to give it a fresh coat of paint and hang the gate on shiny new hinges."

§§§

That week Steve Hastings baptized five of us in the little river in Felton. There were Cyndie and Susan, who had both been saved only very recently; there was Marilyn, who had gotten saved at the same altar as I had on Sunday morning; and then there were Patrick and myself. I could not believe how happy I was in Christ and what an adventure it was to serve Jesus. I was certainly a new creature! And new also was everything I thought and spoke and did. In fact, the whole creation seemed new as I started up the shining way that leads to heaven. Mother Nature was cleaner and brighter, God's love was bathing my soul, and life was abundantly worth living. Knowing God personally through the blood of Jesus Christ was far beyond what I had dreamed it might be. I was in a mood of astonishment for weeks.

Steve and I went to see Bob and his girlfriend in Ben Lomond three or four times, but could not get them to come to Glory Hill, even for a meal. It was all different now between Bob and me, something cold had come in. I tried to be his friend, and prayed much that he would get saved, but we just drifted farther apart. One day he called on the phone and asked if Steve and I would give him a ride out to the north end of Santa Cruz where he could start hitchhiking back toward Canada.

We drove over and picked him up. My dear old friend. He got in the back seat with his traveling gear. My heart was heavy. I tried to express to him how good it was to be saved.

Half way down the mountain Steve pulled over and we prayed for him. He had turned down our fervent invitations to come spend some time at the Walraths'. Nothing would change him. We waved good-bye as he stood out on Pacific Coast Highway with his thumb up, heading for British Columbia.

Life at Glory Hill was everything I needed to help me on my way spiritually. Along with private devotions, family prayer, and a continual revival atmosphere, came the chores and work details. I enjoyed cleaning the gutters and down-spouts in preparation for winter. It was a delight to straighten the barn and haul hay from the feed store in Scott's Valley.

One Saturday, Patrick and I were killing chickens, while Wally and Keith stood at the kitchen sink cleaning and bagging them for the freezer. We had forty or more to kill and pluck, and were having the time of our lives. We had an old stump with two nails sticking up where one of us would hook the head, while the other swung the axe. We were getting tickled at the eyeball staring at us, and blinking after the head was lopped off. Sometimes the beak would strive to talk to us. But we were getting less tickled all the time with having to pluck the wet, smelly feathers off the hot-dipped bodies. It was getting to be too much like work. They smelled like wet dog and stuck to our hands and clothing like steamy goo.

Soon it came my turn to enter the coop and grab a couple of hens. The first thing I noticed was my newly shined boots sinking in the manure. I tried to tiptoe, but there was no hope of ever keeping them clean. I was tempted to back out the door, but I knew it was only fair to share in the labor.

The hens were bobbing and clucking as I began to approach. I had never grabbed a chicken before and had no idea whether to sneak up or plunge. Sneaking didn't seem to be working. I plunged. She dodged, pelting me with filth. I lunged at another and she flopped away, throwing more manure on my face and clothes. Something sprang up in me akin to the devil and I started toward the end of the coop where twenty or more chickens milled restlessly. My boots were covered, my face was speckled and I was mad.

I drove them back into a corner and started grabbing furiously at this one and then that. Their violent flapping broke a window, and all twenty flew squawking and cackling across the hill. I came out of the coop on a dead run. The first thing I could get my hands on was a thin board about three feet long. I raced across the hill, swinging like a wild man. Finally I cornered a red hen against the outside of the coop. She was dodging and ducking and cackling in terror as I clobbered her again and again. I killed the little red hen. When I stretched her across the chopping block her poor wings were limp.

With the fury over and I sat plucking the bruised body. I began to feel like a fool. Then I realized I was learning a lesson. That was carnality! Inherited Sin! That awful, hateful fiend that sprang up in my soul was the sin nature they had been telling me about. Ugly it was, and shameful. Explosive and destructive. As I plucked, I prayed for forgiveness, and for help in dealing with my old nature.

173

That next Sunday, Steve preached on entire sanctification and I hit the altar. I knew if I did not get that awful thing out of my heart I would never last as a Christian. My long hair had already gone by the wayside, my Indian jewelry had been discarded, and the patched blue jeans had gone out with the trash. But my carnal nature was still on board.

God's sanctified people prayed for me and held my feet to the fire. They pointed out that where my getting saved had delivered me from guilt and condemnation, the further work of sanctification would deliver me from unholy tempers and appetites still residing in my soul. My sinful acts had been forgiven, but now my inherited sinful nature must be cleansed. The sin principle, carnality, had to be crucified. Self had to die. I must be filled with the Holy Ghost.

The Bible was clear. The teaching was clear. "For this is the will of God, even your sanctification." That made more sense to me than anything I had ever heard.

I became a regular seeker after heart holiness. One night while at the altar, I ran smack into a piece of blue plastic drain pipe. Doris's drain pipe. "Lord, I see my need of a sanctified heart. I know I'm carnal, Lord, I need Your cleansing."

Blue plastic drain pipe.

"Lord, what can I do? I can't even remember where I left it." I had left it somewhere between Santa Cruz and the Mojave Desert when we had gone to move Tom's mother.

"You will have to pay her for it," said the Still Small Voice.

"I don't know what it's worth."

"Five dollars ought to cover it," He said.

Then, the awfulness of the thing hit me. Doris! Doris Tye. I would have to go up to Doris's house and beg forgiveness and pay for the pipe. I broke out into a cold sweat. Anybody but Doris! And with my short haircut. I was still kneeling at the altar and I could hear her voice, "Who cares about that bunch of crazy Christians! All they want to do is go up there and pray anyway!" I tried to argue, but I knew it was no use. I knew if I was to please God I would have to make the restitution.

The next morning Steve and Pat drove me over to Felton and into Doris Tye's lane. I walked up the steps to the back door. My hands were cold. My whole body was trembling.

174

Knock, knock!

"Come in!"

I opened the door. She was standing at the sink.

"Brad!" She took a step backwards, and looked at me as if to say, 'What happened to you?'

I smiled shyly and looked past her.

"How've you been?" she smiled.

"Pretty good," I cleared my throat. "I've come to pay for something I stole when I left here."

"Really? What was it?"

I tried to describe the blue plastic drain pipe, but she had no idea what I was talking about. I could see the whole thing was putting her more and more in a fog.

I swallowed hard, seeking courage. "I got saved a few weeks ago, and I want to pay for it. I think five dollars would cover it."

"Oh, forget the five dollars," she said heartily. "You got saved? Just lately? I thought you looked different."

But she did not scoff. Big tears filled her eyes. She was silent for a long moment, then she said, "I wish my boys could see you now. They're both in jail over in Sacramento for selling cocaine."

I didn't know what to say. The clock on the wall was ticking.

"You got saved. . ." she said again softly. "Brad, I wish you could talk to them. They really need help."

Doris Tye suddenly changed from an old hippy into a tender-hearted mother. She encouraged me all she possibly could before I walked down the steps and across the lane. My heart was pounding, not in dread, but in overcoming joy.

§§§

Evangelist Ken Fay arrived in December for a revival meeting and I was at the altar every night seeking a pure heart. He was preaching what I had already been introduced to as the "death route." More and more clearly did I see my need of the baptism of the Holy Ghost.

One night while at the altar I heard that Still Small Voice, which I had come to love and follow with all my heart. "Crawl over the altar on your hands and knees," He whispered.

I kept seeking.

"Crawl over the altar," He sweetly urged.

I stopped. Could it possibly be the voice of God? I went back to seeking.

"Crawl over the altar on your hands and knees," He repeated tenderly.

"Lord, is that You?"

"It's Me," He said. "Now, do as I say."

It just could not be God. It was so unlike Him. It must be the enemy.

He continued patiently, "Crawl over the altar, Brad."

"Lord, I'm about to do it," I said in all honesty. "If You keep on, I'm going to do it." I just couldn't believe God would want me to do something so silly.

"Well, do it, then. It is Me. You don't have to understand. Just go. I'll take care of the rest."

Over I went on hands and knees. I laid down on my stomach on the platform with my nose against the carpet. "OK," I prayed, "I did it."

After a moment of tender silence Jesus whispered, "You are on the platform. Behind the pulpit."

"Yes."

"This is where I want you for the rest of your life," He said. "I want you to be a preacher." And then God blessed me so powerfully, I was convinced He had sanctified me at the same time he called me to preach. I just lay there and grinned and blew my nose and had myself a time.

I didn't know enough to say No to the call to preach. I just figured God knew what He was doing, and I was making it my habit to say Yes to everything He desired of me.

God was ordering my life so perfectly that I was in continual wonderment. I was soon making plans to go to Bible Missionary Institute in Rock Island, Illinois, to begin studying for the ministry.

Steve Hastings and I were spending most of our time calling on hippies and doing the various jobs and errands he might happen to be involved in. One evening we were up at the

University making a call on a student. Steve introduced me to Carl and sort of testified for me. Before long, Carl was asking me this and that about the church, the Walrath home, and other things Steve had already been telling him about. I was completely unassuming, and before I realized it, I had been backed into an intellectual corner and was receiving a real needling. He asked me a couple of theological questions I could not answer. Then after he had me in an obvious state of humiliation, he jabbed mockingly, "I guess they're going to ship you off to their Bible College in Rock Island next, huh?"

Like lightening, an ugly flash of hate sprang up in me and I almost slugged him — but I held it down. My heart was pounding wildly. I did not say a word, but just looked off across the campus startled and silent.

Steve and Carl went on talking, unaware of what was going on in my breast. But I was feeling the wrath of carnal anger and the gloom of spiritual disappointment.

We said good-bye to Carl, and were driving down across the big campus meadow, when I said, "Steve, you know when he asked me that stuff about the church, and about BMI?"

"Yes, what about it?"

I told him what had happened inside me, and that I had almost hit him. "Do you think I'm sanctified?" I asked.

"I don't know, Brad," he answered tactfully. "You probably need to pray about it."

Before his big white car pulled up the Glory Hill driveway I knew I was still carnal. When God had called me to preach, I had gotten blessed and had taken it for being filled with the Holy Ghost. Now the Lord showed me that He had never sanctified me. But He also encouraged me to take heart, for He loved me and was pleased with my spiritual progress.

That Sunday in church, we were singing the hymn, "How the Fire Fell." I was singing right along, "Oh, I love to tell the blessed story since the Lord. . ." I could not finish it.

"For my soul received a flood of glory when the Lord. . ." I wasn't sanctified and I wasn't going to sing it. I got angry.

Jesus poked me in the side, "Sing it," He said.

"I'm not sanctified."

"That's right," He said firmly, "but you'll sing it anyway,

just as if you were."

An awful wave of bitterness swept over me. I was pouting. I was not sanctified and it made me mad. Grudgingly I obeyed — "Oh, I never shall forget how the fire fell when the Lord — sanctified me."

I got under such terrible conviction for heart holiness, and developed such a hunger to be cleansed, that my middle name became "Seeker." I was in every prayer meeting and every open altar praying for a pure heart. In my private devotions and in much of my extra time I was seeking deliverance from the carnal self that tormented my inner soul and rendered my Christian testimony weak and incomplete. And everywhere I went, there I was to spoil it all.

I finally took my sleeping bag and hiked to the top of the mountain to fast and pray. God faithfully kept giving me new light, showing me through His Word and through personal experience how desperate was my need. For three days, I read the Word and prayed and slept under the stars. I hiked the ridges, fought the devil, preached to the trees, and moved up the road toward Pentecost.

That next Sunday morning at church the Lord said, "Brad, I want you to get rid of those two female figurines you made in college."

"Lord, that's some of my best work."

"It may be your best sculpture, but it is not the best subject matter."

They had never been intended to be sensual. I was proud of the workmanship, but I could see they would never glorify a holy God. Later that day I got them out of the toolshed where they had been stored along with the rest of my things. I was turning the sculptures into driveway gravel with a sixteen pound sledge hammer when the Lord broke in, "And by the way," He said, "while we're at it, let's get rid of the Zoop-Zoop Man as well."

"But Lord," I protested, "there's nothing immodest about the Zoop-Zoop Man."

The Zoop-Zoop Man was also a piece of sculpture, the only other piece from my college days that I had felt worth keeping. I was not that good at sculpting and I had formed the mouth in such a way as to make him look like he was saying, "Zoop." The striking thing about the Zoop-Zoop Man was that he looked just like me. I had not intended it so, it had just turned out that way, a common occurrence with untalented sculptors.

"Lord," I argued, "he looks just like me."

"Yes, and that is just the problem," He answered. "and you have to die."

I stood him out on the driveway, took one last look, and swung the sledge with a death blow to his head.

The Walrath farmhouse sat in the midst of steep rumpled hills and sharp little valleys. About a quarter of a mile away was a broken-down cabin deep in the redwoods. I was in that cabin one afternoon seeking the Holy Ghost and was in the spirit of prayer when the Lord stopped me. "Wait a minute," He gently urged. "Brad, what do you want?"

"I want to be sanctified," I replied.

"Now — " He persisted, kindly but firmly, "what do you really want?"

I've always tried to be completely honest with God. Only a fool would try to be anything else with Omniscience. "I want a wife," I admitted. "I want a wife who will love You more than she loves me."

Jesus said, "I just wanted you to know that I have My eye on her this very moment." I knew He was smiling. "If you follow Me perfectly, I promise I will lead you right to her." Then, as is His way it seems, He blessed so good that I shouted and cried all over the deserted cabin and out into the woods.

"Lord, how will I know her?"

"I'll worry about that," He promised. "You just keep step with me, that is all you have to do."

§§§

At first my parents had been skeptical concerning my new change in life. They had seen me go through a lot of changes in the last few years, and over the phone this probably sounded like just another crazy idea. During the Christmas season they traveled up to Santa Cruz to visit me, and meet the people I'd been telling them about over the phone. After coming to the Walraths' home and seeing what I was involved in for themselves, they were convinced. In fact they were thrilled to see their son clean-cut, clear-eyed, and happily planning a legitimate future. They were so happy about the great change the Lord had made in me that they wanted to pay my tuition to Bible College so I would have enough time to get good grades and keep on top spiritually.

That January, 1972, four of us from Santa Cruz took off for Bible Missionary Institute. We drove out across Interstate 80 through snow and ice, trading off driving, and pulled into Davenport, Iowa in just over forty-eight hours. We called Steven and Sandy Palm from a gas station and they led us to their house which was next door to their church. After a night with them, Steven Palm drove us across the Mississippi River and up to the campus.

I was as green as they came, I had only been saved three months. The world I walked into at Bible School was a veritable wonderland in my eyes. "The Hill" upon which the college sat was like a holy island in the middle of a world of sin. The people who lived and worked there were more of the same kind of saints I had already found the Walraths and Steve Hastings to be. During registration day, I got in a line of students heading through the administration offices. By the time the line had brought me up to the office doors, I had met the girl of my promise. I was keeping step with the will of God, and I stepped right in line behind Joan Haggins. After we had been talking for a few minutes I found out she was a Canadian from Ontario. I was trying to appear casual and nonchalant, but by the time the registration line had crawled up the stairs to the Dean's office, I was so excited that I had to quit the line and seek out my new friends in the dorm.

I happily informed the guys that I had just met Joan Haggins, and was pleased to hear that she was one of the most spiritual girls at school that year. I started praying, I did not want to make any mistakes. God had promised He would bring that special one along and I was making sure I did not have my wires crossed.

I prayed for two weeks. Everybody in school knew I was praying about Joan. She knew it, too. But that was all right. I was not going to ask a girl to have lunch with me unless I knew she was the one God had for me. I wasn't interested in a date. I was twenty-four years old; I wanted a wife, and I wanted God's choice.

At BMI I had walked into a powerful revival atmosphere, and I had gone to seeking holiness just that much more diligently. No one but the Lord will ever know what a blessing Bible Missionary Institute was to my soul. The faculty, the students, the churches, the spirit of prayer and seeking God — these were all factors in my rapid spiritual development. The curriculum was almost a devotional life of its own for me. The spiritual food and fellowship were all my soul could have desired.

Along with sanctification, I was also seeking God's will concerning Joan. I prayed through on Joan first. We started having meals together in the school dining room. I didn't have any trouble getting sanctified when it came to our relationship because I had given her over to God in consecration before I ever asked for a date.

It finally came to the place where the only trouble I was having getting sanctified was faith. Evangelist E. E. Michael was preaching a revival in Davenport, my home church, and I had been at the altar every night. But the praying was all prayed. The death route was behind me. I was consecrated, on the altar, and dead as far as a man could die. But the "route" does not sanctify. Crucifixion of the carnal nature is an act of God. I had to trust God to sanctify me through His truth, I had to take Him at His word.

Besides preaching in the Davenport church every night, Brother Michael was also preaching in chapel every day at the college. One morning, I walked into chapel and something unusual was happening; everybody was standing in silence and awe. None of the faculty or Brother Michael had come in yet, but God was on the scene so mightily that no one would sit down. The hallway outside the chapel was a rush of hubbub and chaos with the changing of class. But as the students stepped into the chapel, each was immediately impressed with holy reverence. All was silent and glorious. The piano and organ began softly. Someone in the congregation started to sing and we all joined softly in the song of praise and adoration. Soon the staff arrived. The college president, B. M. Loftin, stepped to the pulpit. All went quiet. "We don't need to go any further this morning. God is here," he smiled. "If you have a need in your heart, this would be a good time to pray it through."

The chapel seats began to empty as the students moved to

the aisles and toward the front. A full thirty percent of the student body gathered around the altar area to pray. By the time I reached the front, the platform and altar were filled with seekers. The first two rows of chairs were filled, and every available space was occupied by a kneeling student. I looked around for a place to kneel. I decided if I was going to get any closer to the front, I would have to step over some seekers and lie down under the piano, that was the only empty space I could see.

I had learned enough by now, and I was perfectly satisfied that I had gotten to the "end of self " in my seeking. When I got situated between the piano bench and the piano, I patiently and hopefully prayed the same prayer I had been praying for the last three days and three nights, "Lord, I'm here to be sanctified." And that was it. Any other praying would have been redundant. I was all on the altar and now it was up to God. I waited.

God was on the scene mightily, but after a few moments I was aware that He was under the piano in a special way. He had come down to where I was and was encamped upon my very soul.

"It's the Holy Ghost," I said to myself. When I acknowledged Him, He settled right on me. "It is the Holy Ghost! He is right here over me."

"NO!" screamed the devil. "It's not the Holy Ghost!"

"It is the Holy Ghost," I resisted, and with that the Spirit of God came even nearer. "It's the Holy Ghost, and He has come to sanctify me."

"NO! NO!" Satan yelled. "IT'S NOT HIM. HE'S NOT GOING TO SANCTIFY YOU!"

"Of course it's him," I contended. I would have been lying to have said otherwise.

"He's not going to sanctify you!" shouted the enemy.

"Well, sure He is," I was positive. "That's what He's here for." And in that moment the Spirit of God slipped silently into my heart.

Satan murmured something unintelligible and departed.

I lay there for a long moment. The Person of the Holy Ghost and I were occupying the same space. He had come into me. I had no special feeling, I just knew He was there — we were dwelling in the same location.

Finally God asked, "Did I sanctify you?"

"Yes, Lord."

"Are you sure, now?" He said sweetly.

"Yes, Lord, I'm sure."

"Well," He seemed to say, "why don't you get out from under the piano?"

I started to get up, but before I found my feet, the glory struck my soul, and I had to hold on to the corners of the piano for fear I would bounce off through the crowded altar area. I could never describe how I felt, but how I felt is not so important as the actual work that was done. My heart was cleansed from inbred sin. In an instant, under that piano, my nature was changed by the incoming of God's Holy Spirit. The body of sin was eradicated and the Holy Ghost took up residence in my heart. In the vessel which had once echoed for the filling of God, there was now a resonating harmony as creature and Creator came together in one.

I was shouting. I could remain still no longer. I let go of the piano, ran across the front of the platform to the other side of the chapel, repelled off the far wall, and ran back across to the piano and grabbed hold. I was astonished, I looked around. A solid line of people were praying, filling both sides of the altar, and all the platform, and all the floor space everywhere I looked. There was not one spot in which to step where there were not arms and legs and bodies and heads of kneeling souls. I had touched no one. I know I didn't fly, but where I stepped I'll never know.

§§§

During that spring Semester Joan and I were engaged. By the time school had resumed for the fall we were married and living in a little house-trailer in Coal Valley. This is not supposed to be a love story, but I would like to say that falling in love and being engaged at Bible College, and keeping all the dating rules, was a joy beyond description. Those were some of the greatest days I ever hope to live on earth. Being in love with someone in Jesus Christ is a blessed and holy thing, regal in quality and pure as driven snow.

After we got married, I attended school until the spring of 1974. Then, in keeping with the will of God, Joan and I, and our baby Christopher, headed out to Santa Cruz, California.

That first Sunday morning back in Santa Cruz I was thrilled to take Joan to the little church where I had been saved some two and a half years earlier. I showed her the very spot where I had been kneeling when salvation first entered my soul. We enjoyed the morning service worshiping with many of my old friends and also many new ones.

In the two and a half years since I had been gone, Steve Hastings had moved to Oakland, California, where he was working full-time and preaching in a church and rescue mission. The Walraths' ministry had changed drastically. Wally had resigned his job in Palo Alto and moved the entire Glory Hill work into a large resort-type property which was fondly referred to as the "Shepherd's Fold." They were feeding as many as twenty-five people three meals a day by faith. The Elm Street Gospel Mission had been opened to provide the Shepherd's Fold with a direct work among the street people. And the Bible Missionary Church was running close to a hundred in attendance.

When the service was over on that first Sunday morning, everyone was visiting. I just had to have a look around, so I walked quietly down the church steps alone, and started for a stroll down the block. But I had only gone across the alley when I had to stop. Lo and behold, the fence! I had forgotten all about the fence, and there it was, looking like brand new. It was straight and strong and solid. It had been scraped, sanded and painted, and it now enclosed a beautiful little yard with flowers and vegetables mingled around the perimeter. I walked over to the gate and saw that it had been perfectly restored and hung on shiny new hinges. I could not resist. I tripped the latch and let it swing open freely. Not a squeak. I closed it with a "click" and examined the main gatepost where I had once chipped the aging paint with my fingernail. It was as smooth as new could have made it, and as white as the sunshine on that fine spring day.

The Lord stepped near and smiled. "That's the way I feel about it, Brad," He whispered. "You've come a long way, and I'm pleased."

Then He took me by the arm. "Come on," He said, "let's take a walk around the block."

THE END

184

Commanding General
Fort Ord, Calif.   93941

Dear Sir:

In November, 1969 I was drafted into the Army and stationed at Fort Ord. At that time I was a typical, rebellious youth taking drugs and hating the establishment. I purposed in myself to do all I could to get out of the Army.

I was sent to Fort Eustis, VA for my A.I.T. when I began my intensified efforts to get discharged. My medical history was rich with psychiatrists and drugs and I began using this as a tool. In the few months that followed I lied, went AWOL, faked suicide, damaged U.S. property, and stole U.S. property. I was discharged in June, 1970 on medical grounds concerning my mental make-up.

Since that time I've been saved. I found Jesus in October, 1971. I confessed my sins and repented; I asked His forgiveness and He faithfully saved me from my sins. I've been in Santa Cruz since April of this year after attending our Church Bible College in Illinois for the past two years. I am a minister here with the Christian Anti-Narcotic Association and the acting assistant pastor of the local Bible Missionary Church.

In drawing closer to the Lord in a recent revival I am impressed to make this restitution. I find in the Bible where it says Mt. 5:22-23, "Therefore if thou bring thy gift to the altar, and there rememberest that thy brother has ought against thee; leave there thy gift before the altar, and go thy way; first be reconciled to thy brother, and then come and offer thy gift." God has impressed me to make this apology and restitution now if I would maintain my growth in His kingdom.

I humbly apologize for my attitudes toward our country and more specifically to the U.S. Army. I ask your forgiveness for my deceitfulness in dealing with the Army.

When in Ft. Eustis I defaced a small barracks room with house paint of various colors. When AWOL from Ft. Ord S.P.D. I left a new field jacket and a pair of combat boots at home for later use.

If you will let me know the current value of a field jacket and boots (as are issued to new trainees) I will send you a check for the amount. Concerning the room I defaced in Ft. Eustis, I will be happy to pay the bill on its repairs.

I commit myself to your mercy and judgment regarding my deceitful conduct. Thanking you for your attention I remain,

The Servant of our Lord,

H. Bradford Henshaw

See next page for Army's response.

DEPARTMENT OF THE ARMY

HEADQUARTERS

UNITED STATES ARMY TRAINING CENTER AND 7TH INFANTRY DIVISION

FORT ORD, CALIFORNIA 93941

ATZO-AG-FZ

1 NOV 1974

Mr. H. Bradford Henshaw
1324 El Rancho Drive
Santa Cruz, California 95060

Dear Mr. Henshaw:

This is in reply to your letter regarding restitution to the Army for a field jacket, a pair of boots and the damage caused to a small barracks room.

It was with pleasure that I read your letter and learned of your new goals in life. Your apology is accepted and your alleged debts to the United States Army are forgiven.

I trust this will bring you peace of mind, and wish you success in your future endeavors.

Sincerely,

W. A. SLAUGHTER
Captain, AGC
Assistant Adjutant General

Bradford Henshaw was raised in a middle-class American home. In the 1960's he attended Long Beach State College as an art student. After a short stint in the Army he traveled with the hippies in a desperate search for Reality. At the age of twenty four, he encountered the person of Jesus Christ, and discovered the reason for living.

He then attended Bible College, met and married Joan Haggins, and in 1974 they entered full-time ministry. Brad has pastored a number of churches across the United States and Canada, served as a missionary in British Columbia, and has traveled extensively as an evangelist.

The story of Brad's search for God can be found in his book, *The Rocks Cried Out*. His second book, *Broken Angel*, tells of Joan's final harrowing journey to the gate of heaven.

To order books or contact Brad:
AldenTowersLibrary@gmail.com

Made in the USA
Columbia, SC
24 May 2018